Real Soldiers of Fortune

Richard Harding Davis

Real Soldiers of Fortune

Richard Harding Davis

© 1st World Library – Literary Society, 2004
PO Box 2211
Fairfield, IA 52556
www.1stworldlibrary.org
First Edition

LCCN: 2004091268

Softcover ISBN: 1-59540-686-7
eBook ISBN: 1-59540-786-3

Purchase *"Real Soldiers of Fortune"*
as a traditional bound book at:
www.1stWorldLibrary.org/purchase.asp?ISBN=1-59540-686-7

1st World Library Literary Society is a nonprofit organization dedicated to promoting literacy by:

- Creating a free internet library accessible from any computer worldwide.
- Hosting writing competitions and offering book publishing scholarships.

Readers interested in supporting literacy through sponsorship, donations or membership please contact:
literacy@1stworldlibrary.org
Check us out at: www.1stworldlibrary.org

Real Soldiers of Fortune
contributed by the Charles Family
in support of
1st World Library Literary Society

MAJOR-GENERAL HENRY RONALD DOUGLAS MACIVER

ANY sunny afternoon, on Fifth Avenue, or at night in the *table d'hote* restaurants of University Place, you may meet the soldier of fortune who of all his brothers in arms now living is the most remarkable. You may have noticed him; a stiffly erect, distinguished-looking man, with gray hair, an imperial of the fashion of Louis Napoleon, fierce blue eyes, and across his forehead a sabre cut.

This is Henry Ronald Douglas MacIver, for some time in India an ensign in the Sepoy mutiny; in Italy, lieutenant under Garibaldi; in Spain, captain under Don Carlos; in our Civil War, major in the Confederate army; in Mexico, lieutenant-colonel under the Emperor Maximilian; colonel under Napoleon III, inspector of cavalry for the Khedive of Egypt, and chief of cavalry and general of brigade of the army of King Milan of Servia. These are only a few of his military titles. In 1884 was published a book giving the story of his life up to that year. It was called "Under Fourteen Flags." If to-day General MacIver were to reprint the book, it would be called "Under Eighteen Flags."

MacIver was born on Christmas Day, 1841, at sea, a league off the shore of Virginia. His mother was Miss Anna Douglas of that State; Ronald MacIver, his father, was a Scot, a Rossshire gentleman, a younger son of the chief of the Clan MacIver. Until he was ten years old young MacIver played in Virginia at the home of his father. Then, in order that he might be educated, he was shipped to Edinburgh to an uncle, General Donald Graham. After five years his uncle obtained for him a commission as ensign in the Honorable East India Company, and at sixteen, when other boys are preparing for college, MacIver was in the Indian Mutiny, fighting, not for a flag, nor a country, but as one fights a wild animal, for his life. He was wounded in the arm, and, with a sword, cut over the head. As a safeguard against the sun the boy had placed inside his helmet a wet towel. This saved him to fight another day, but even with that protection the sword sank through the helmet, the towel, and into the skull. To-day you can see the scar. He was left in the road for dead, and even after his wounds had healed, was six weeks in the hospital.

This tough handling at the very start might have satisfied some men, but in the very next war MacIver was a volunteer and wore the red shirt of Garibaldi. He remained at the front throughout that campaign, and until within a few years there has been no campaign of consequence in which he has not taken part. He served in the Ten Years' War in Cuba, in Brazil, in Argentina, in Crete, in Greece, twice in Spain in Carlist revolutions, in Bosnia, and for four years in our Civil War under Generals Jackson and Stuart around Richmond. In this great war he was four times wounded.

It was after the surrender of the Confederate army, that, with other Southern officers, he served under Maximilian in Mexico; in Egypt, and in France.

Whenever in any part of the world there was fighting, or the rumor of fighting, the procedure of the general invariably was the same. He would order himself to instantly depart for the front, and on arriving there would offer to organize a foreign legion. The command of this organization always was given to him. But the foreign legion was merely the entering wedge. He would soon show that he was fitted for a better command than a band of undisciplined volunteers, and would receive a commission in the regular army. In almost every command in which he served that is the manner in which promotion came. Sometimes he saw but little fighting, sometimes he should have died several deaths, each of a nature more unpleasant than the others. For in war the obvious danger of a bullet is but a three hundred to one shot, while in the pack against the combatant the jokers are innumerable. And in the career of the general the unforeseen adventures are the most interesting. A man who in eighteen campaigns has played his part would seem to have earned exemption from any other risks, but often it was outside the battle-field that MacIver encountered the greatest danger. He fought several duels, in two of which he killed his adversary; several attempts were made to assassinate him, and while on his way to Mexico he was captured by hostile Indians. On returning from an expedition in Cuba he was cast adrift in an open boat and for days was without food.

Long before I met General MacIver I had read his book and had heard of him from many men who had met him in many different lands while engaged in as many different undertakings. Several of the older war correspondents knew him intimately; Bennett Burleigh of the *Telegraph* was his friend, and E. F. Knight of the *Times* was one of those who volunteered for a filibustering expedition which MacIver organized against New Guinea. The late Colonel Ochiltree of Texas told me tales of MacIver's bravery, when as young men they were fellow officers in the Southern army, and Stephen Bonsal had met him when MacIver was United States Consul at Denia in Spain. When MacIver arrived at this post, the ex-consul refused to vacate the Consulate, and MacIver wished to settle the difficulty with duelling pistols. As Denia is a small place, the inhabitants feared for their safety, and Bonsal, who was our *charge d'affaires* then, was sent from Madrid to adjust matters. Without bloodshed he got rid of the ex-consul, and later MacIver so endeared himself to the Denians that they begged the State Department to retain him in that place for the remainder of his life.

Before General MacIver was appointed to a high position at the St. Louis Fair, I saw much of him in New York. His room was in a side street in an old-fashioned boarding-house, and overlooked his neighbor's back yard and a typical New York City sumac tree; but when the general talked one forgot he was within a block of the Elevated, and roamed over all the world. On his bed he would spread out wonderful parchments, with strange, heathenish inscriptions, with great seals, with faded ribbons. These were signed by Sultans, Secretaries of War, Emperors, filibusters. They were military commissions, titles of nobility, brevets for decorations, instructions and commands from superior officers. Translated the phrases ran: "Imposing special confidence in," "we appoint," or "create," or "declare," or "In recognition of services rendered to our person," or "country," or "cause," or "For bravery on the field of battle we bestow the Cross - "

As must a soldier, the general travels "light," and all his worldly possessions were crowded ready for mobilization into a small compass. He had his sword, his field blanket, his trunk, and the tin despatch boxes that held his papers. From these, like a conjurer, he would draw souvenirs of all the world. From the embrace of faded letters, he would unfold old photographs, daguerrotypes, and miniatures of fair women and adventurous men: women who now are queens in exile, men who, lifted on waves of absinthe, still, across a *cafe* table, tell how they will win back a crown.

Once in a written document the general did me the honor to appoint me his literary executor, but as he is young, and as healthy as myself, it never may be my lot to perform such an unwelcome duty. And to-day all one can write of him is what the world can read in "Under Fourteen Flags," and some of the "foot-notes to history" which I have copied from his scrap-book. This scrap-book is a wonderful volume, but owing to "political" and other reasons, for the present, of the many clippings from newspapers it contains there are only a few I am at liberty to print. And from them it is difficult to make a choice. To sketch in a few thousand words a career that had developed under Eighteen Flags is in its very wealth embarrassing.

Here is one story, as told by the scrap-book, of an expedition that failed. That it failed was due to a British Cabinet Minister; for had Lord Derby possessed the imagination of the Soldier of Fortune, his Majesty's dominions might now be the richer by many thousands of square miles and many thousands of black subjects.

On October 29, 1883, the following appeared in the London *Standard*: "The New Guinea Exploration and Colonization Company is already chartered, and the first expedition expects to leave before Christmas." "The prospectus states settlers intending to join the first party must contribute one hundred pounds toward the company. This subscription will include all expenses for passage money. Six months' provisions will be provided, together with tents and arms for protection. Each subscriber of one hundred pounds is to obtain a certificate entitling him to one thousand acres."

The view of the colonization scheme taken by the *Times* of London, of the same date, is less complaisant. "The latest commercial sensation is a proposed company for the seizure of New Guinea. Certain adventurous gentlemen are looking out for one hundred others who have money and a taste for buccaneering. When the company has been completed, its share-holders are to place themselves under military regulations, sail in a body for New Guinea, and without asking anybody's leave, seize upon the island and at once, in some unspecified way, proceed to realize large profits. If the idea does not suggest comparisons with the large designs of Sir Francis Drake, it is at least not unworthy of Captain Kidd."

When we remember the manner in which some of the colonies of Great Britain were acquired, the *Times* seems almost squeamish.

In a Melbourne paper, June, 1884, is the following paragraph:

"Toward the latter part of 1883 the Government of

Queensland planted the flag of Great Britain on the shores of New Guinea. When the news reached England it created a sensation. The Earl of Derby, Secretary for the Colonies, refused, however, to sanction the annexation of New Guinea, and in so doing acted contrary to the sincere wish of every right-thinking Anglo-Saxon under the Southern Cross.

"While the subsequent correspondence between the Home and Queensland governments was going on, Brigadier-General H. R. MacIver originated and organized the New Guinea Exploration and Colonization Company in London, with a view to establishing settlements on the island. The company, presided over by General Beresford of the British Army, and having an eminently representative and influential board of directors, had a capital of two hundred and fifty thousand pounds, and placed the supreme command of the expedition in the hands of General MacIver. Notwithstanding the character of the gentlemen composing the board of directors, and the truly peaceful nature of the expedition, his Lordship informed General MacIver that in the event of the latter's attempting to land on New Guinea, instructions would be sent to the officer in command of her Majesty's fleet in the Western Pacific to fire upon the company's vessel. This meant that the expedition would be dealt with as a filibustering one.

In *Judy*, September 21, 1887, appears:

"We all recollect the treatment received by Brigadier-General MacI. in the action he took with respect to the annexation of New Guinea. The General, who is a sort of Pizarro, with a dash of D'Artagnan, was treated in a most scurvy manner by Lord Derby. Had MacIver not been thwarted in his enterprise, the whole of New Guinea would now have been under the British flag, and we should not be cheek-by-jowl with the Germans, as we are in too many places."

Society, September 3, 1887, says:

"The New Guinea expedition proved abortive, owing to the blundering shortsightedness of the then Government, for which Lord Derby was chiefly responsible, but what little foothold we possess in New Guinea, is certainly due to General MacIver's gallant effort."

Copy of statement made by J. Rintoul Mitchell, June 2, 1887:

"About the latter end of the year 1883, when I was editor-in-chief of the *Englishman* in Calcutta, I was told by Captain de Deaux, assistant secretary in the Foreign Office of the Indian Government, that he had received a telegram from Lord Derby to the effect that if General MacIver ventured to land upon the coast of New Guinea it would become the duty of Lord Ripon, Viceroy, to use the naval forces at his command for the purpose of deporting General MacI. Sir Aucland Calvin can certify to this, as it was discussed in the Viceregal Council."

Just after our Civil War MacIver was interested in another expedition which also failed. Its members called themselves the Knights of Arabia, and their object was to colonize an island much nearer to our shores than New Guinea. MacIver, saying that his oath prevented, would never tell me which island this was, but the reader can choose from among Cuba, Haiti, and the Hawaiian group. To have taken Cuba, the "colonizers" would have had to fight not only Spain, but the Cubans themselves, on whose side they were soon fighting in the Ten Years' War; so Cuba may be eliminated. And as the expedition was to sail from the Atlantic side, and not from San Francisco, the island would appear to be the Black Republic. From the records of the times it would seem that the greater number of the Knights of Arabia were veterans of the Confederate army, and there is no question but that they intended to subjugate the blacks of Haiti and form a republic for white men in which slavery would be recognized. As one of the leaders of this filibustering expedition, MacIver was arrested by General Phil Sheridan and for a short time cast into jail.

This chafed the general's spirit, but he argued philosophically that imprisonment for filibustering, while irksome, brought with it no reproach. And, indeed, sometimes the only difference between a filibuster and a government lies in the fact that the government fights the gun-boats of only the enemy while a filibuster must dodge the boats of the enemy and those of his own countrymen. When the United States went to war with Spain there were many men in jail as filibusters, for doing that which at the time the country secretly approved, and later imitated. And because they attempted exactly the same thing for which Dr. Jameson was imprisoned in Holloway Jail, two hundred thousand of his countrymen are now wearing medals.

The by-laws of the Knights of Arabia leave but little doubt as to its object.

By-law No. II reads:

"We, as Knights of Arabia, pledge ourselves to aid, comfort, and protect all Knights of Arabia, especially those who are wounded in obtaining our grand object.

"III - Great care must be taken that no unbeliever or outsider shall gain any insight into the mysteries or secrets of the Order.

"IV - The candidate will have to pay one hundred dollars cash to the Captain of the Company, and the candidate will receive from the Secretary a Knight of Arabia bond for one hundred dollars in gold, with ten per cent interest, payable ninety days after the recognition of (The Republic of -) by the United States, or any government.

"V - All Knights of Arabia will be entitled to one hundred acres of land, location of said land to be drawn for by lottery. The products are coffee, sugar, tobacco, and cotton."

A local correspondent of the New York *Herald* writes of the arrest of MacIver as follows:

"When MacIver will be tried is at present unknown, as his case has assumed a complicated aspect. He claims British protection as a subject of her British Majesty, and the English Consul has forwarded a statement of his case to Sir Frederick Bruce at Washington, accompanied by a copy of the by-laws. General Sheridan also has forwarded a statement to the Secretary of War, accompanied not only by the by-laws, but very important documents, including letters from Jefferson Davis, Benjamin, the Secretary of State of the Confederate States, and other personages prominent in the Rebellion, showing that MacIver enjoyed the highest confidence of the Confederacy."

As to the last statement, an open letter I found in his scrap-book is an excellent proof. It is as follows: "To officers and members of all camps of United Confederate Veterans: It affords me the greatest pleasure to say that the bearer of this letter, General Henry Ronald MacIver, was an officer of great gallantry in the Confederate Army, serving on the staff at various times of General Stonewall Jackson, J. E. B. Stuart, and E. Kirby Smith, and that his official record is one of which any man may be proud.

"Respectfully, MARCUS J. WRIGHT,
"*Agent for the Collection of Confederate Records.*

"War Records office, War Department, Washington, July 8, 1895."

At the close of the war duels between officers of the two armies were not infrequent. In the scrap-book there is the account of one of these affairs sent from Vicksburg to a Northern paper by a correspondent who was an eye-witness of the event. It tells how Major MacIver, accompanied by Major Gillespie, met, just outside of Vicksburg, Captain Tomlin of Vermont, of the United States Artillery Volunteers. The duel was with swords. MacIver ran Tomlin through the body. The correspondent writes:

"The Confederate officer wiped his sword on his handkerchief. In a few seconds Captain Tomlin expired. One of Major MacIver's seconds called to him: 'He is dead; you must go. These gentlemen will look after the body of their friend.' A negro boy brought up the horses, but before mounting MacIver said to Captain Tomlin's seconds: 'My friends are in haste for me to go. Is there anything I can do? I hope you consider that this matter has been settled honorably?'

"There being no reply, the Confederates rode away."

In a newspaper of to-day so matter-of-fact an acceptance of an event so tragic would make strange reading.

From the South MacIver crossed through Texas to join the Royalist army under the Emperor Maximilian. It was while making his way, with other Confederate officers, from Galveston to El Paso, that MacIver was captured by the Indians. He was not ill-treated by them, but for three months was a prisoner, until one night, the Indians having camped near the Rio Grande, he escaped into Mexico. There he offered his sword to the Royalist commander, General Mejia, who placed him on his staff, and showed him some few skirmishes. At Monterey MacIver saw big fighting, and for his share in it received the title of Count, and the order of Guadaloupe. In June, contrary to all rules of civilized war, Maximilian was executed and the empire was at an end. MacIver escaped to the coast, and from Tampico took a sailing vessel to Rio de Janeiro. Two months later he was wearing the uniform of another emperor, Dom Pedro, and, with the rank of lieutenant-colonel, was in command of the Foreign Legion of the armies of Brazil and Argentina, which at that time as allies were fighting against Paraguay.

MacIver soon recruited seven hundred men, but only half of these ever reached the front. In Buenos Ayres cholera broke out and thirty thousand people died, among the number about half the Legion. MacIver was among those who suffered, and before he recovered was six weeks in hospital. During that period, under a junior officer, the Foreign Legion was sent to the front, where it was disbanded.

On his return to Glasgow, MacIver foregathered with an old friend, Bennett Burleigh, whom he had known when Burleigh was a lieutenant in the navy of the Confederate States. Although today known as a distinguished war correspondent, in those days Burleigh was something of a soldier of fortune himself, and was organizing an expedition to assist the Cretan insurgents against the Turks. Between the two men it was arranged that MacIver should precede the expedition to Crete and prepare for its arrival. The Cretans received him gladly, and from the provisional government he received a commission in which he was given "full power to make war on land and sea against the enemies of Crete, and particularly against the Sultan of Turkey and the Turkish forces, and to burn, destroy, or capture any vessel bearing the Turkish flag."

This permission to destroy the Turkish navy single-handed strikes one as more than generous, for the Cretans had no navy, and before one could begin the destruction of a Turkish gun-boat it was first necessary to catch it and tie it to a wharf.

At the close of the Cretan insurrection MacIver crossed to Athens and served against the brigands in Kisissia on the borders of Albania and Thessaly as volunteer aide to Colonel Corroneus, who had been commander-in-chief of the Cretans against the Turks. MacIver spent three months potting at brigands, and for his services in the mountains was recommended for the highest Greek decoration.

From Greece it was only a step to New York, and almost immediately MacIver appears as one of the Goicouria-Christo expedition to Cuba, of which Goicouria was commander-in-chief, and two famous American officers, Brigadier-General Samuel C. Williams was a general and Colonel Wright Schumburg was chief of staff.

In the scrap-book I find "General Order No. 11 of the Liberal Army of the Republic of Cuba, issued at Cedar Keys, October 3, 1869." In it Colonel MacIver is spoken of as in charge of officers not attached to any organized corps of the division. And again:

"General Order No. V, Expeditionary Division, Republic of Cuba, on board *Lilian*," announces that the place to which the expedition is bound has been changed, and that General Wright Schumburg, who now is in command, orders "all officers not otherwise commissioned to join Colonel MacIver's 'Corps of Officers.'"

The *Lilian* ran out of coal, and to obtain firewood put in at Cedar Keys. For two weeks the patriots cut wood and drilled upon the beach, when they were captured by a British gun-boat and taken to Nassau. There they were set at liberty, but their arms, boat, and stores were confiscated.

In a sailing vessel MacIver finally reached Cuba, and under Goicouria, who had made a successful landing, saw some "help yourself" fighting. Goicouria's force was finally scattered, and MacIver escaped from the Spanish soldiery only by putting to sea in an open boat, in which he endeavored to make Jamaica.

On the third day out he was picked up by a steamer and again landed at Nassau, from which place he returned to New York.

At that time in this city there was a very interesting man named Thaddeus P. Mott, who had been an officer in our army and later had entered the service of Ismail Pasha. By the Khedive he had been appointed a general of division and had received permission to reorganize the Egyptian army.

His object in coming to New York was to engage officers for that service. He came at an opportune moment. At that time the city was filled with men who, in the Rebellion, on one side or the other, had held command, and many of these, unfitted by four years of soldiering for any other calling, readily accepted the commissions which Mott had authority to offer. New York was not large enough to keep MacIver and Mott long apart, and they soon came to an understanding. The agreement drawn up between them is a curious document. It is written in a neat hand on sheets of foolscap tied together like a Commencement-day address, with blue ribbon. In it MacIver agrees to serve as colonel of cavalry in the service of the Khedive. With a few legal phrases omitted, the document reads as follows:

"Agreement entered into this 24th day of March, 1870, between the Government of his Royal Highness and the Khedive of Egypt, represented by General Thaddeus P. Mott of the first part, and H. R. H.

MacIver of New York City.

"The party of the second part, being desirous of entering into the service of party of the first part, in the military capacity of a colonel of cavalry, promises to serve and obey party of the first part faithfully and truly in his military capacity during the space of five years from this date; that the party of the second part waives all claims of protection usually afforded to Americans by consular and diplomatic agents of the United States, and expressly obligates himself to be subject to the orders of the party of the first part, and to make, wage, and vigorously prosecute war against any and all the enemies of party of the first part; that the party of the second part will not under any event be governed, controlled by, or submit to, any order, law, mandate, or proclamation issued by the Government of the United States of America, forbidding party of the second part to serve party of the first part to make war according to any of the provisions herein contained, *it being, however, distinctly understood* that nothing herein contained shall be construed as obligating party of the second part to bear arms or wage war against the United States of America.

"Party of the first part promises to furnish party of the second part with horses, rations, and pay him for his services the same salary now paid to colonels of cavalry in United States army, and will furnish him quarters suitable to his rank in army. Also promises, in the case of illness caused by climate, that said party may resign his office and shall receive his expenses to America and two months' pay; that he receives one-fifth of his regular pay during his active service, together with all expenses of every nature attending such enterprise."

It also stipulates as to what sums shall be paid his family or children in case of his death.

To this MacIver signs this oath:

"In the presence of the ever-living God, I swear that I will in all things honestly, faithfully, and truly keep, observe, and perform the obligations and promises above enumerated, and endeavor to conform to the wishes and desires of the Government of his Royal Highness, the Khedive of Egypt, in all things connected with the furtherance of his prosperity, and the maintenance of his throne."

On arriving at Cairo, MacIver was appointed inspector-general of cavalry, and furnished with a uniform, of which this is a description: "It consisted of a blue tunic with gold spangles, embroidered in gold up the sleeves and front, neat-fitting red trousers, and high patent-leather boots, while the inevitable fez completed the gay costume."

The climate of Cairo did not agree with MacIver, and, in spite of his "gay costume," after six months he left the Egyptian service. His honorable discharge was signed by Stone Bey, who, in the favor of the Khedive, had supplanted General Mott.

It is a curious fact that, in spite of his ill health, immediately after leaving Cairo, MacIver was sufficiently recovered to at once plunge into the Franco-Prussian War. At the battle of Orleans, while on the staff of General Chanzy, he was wounded. In this war his rank was that of a colonel of cavalry of the auxiliary army.

His next venture was in the Carlist uprising of 1873, when he formed a Carlist League, and on several occasions acted as bearer of important messages from the "King," as Don Carlos was called, to the sympathizers with his cause in France and England.

MacIver was promised, if he carried out successfully a certain mission upon which he was sent, and if Don Carlos became king, that he would be made a marquis. As Don Carlos is still a pretender, MacIver is still a general. Although in disposing of his sword MacIver never allowed his personal predilections to weigh with him, he always treated himself to a hearty dislike of the Turks, and we next find him fighting against them in Herzegovina with the Montenegrins. And when the Servians declared war against the same people, MacIver returned to London to organize a cavalry brigade to fight with the Servian army.

Of this brigade and of the rapid rise of MacIver to highest rank and honors in Servia, the scrap-book is most eloquent. The cavalry brigade was to be called the Knights of the Red Cross.

In a letter to the editor of the *Hour*, the general himself speaks of it in the following terms:

"It may be interesting to many of your readers to learn that a select corps of gentlemen is at present in course of organization under the above title with the mission of proceeding to the Levant to take measures in case of emergency for the defense of the Christian population, and more especially of British subjects who are to a great extent unprovided with adequate means of protection from the religious furies of the Mussulmans. The lives of Christian women and children are in hourly peril from fanatical hordes. The Knights will be carefully chosen and kept within strict military control, and will be under command of a practical soldier with large experience of the Eastern countries. Templars and all other crusaders are invited to give aid and sympathy."

Apparently MacIver was not successful in enlisting many Knights, for a war correspondent at the capital of Servia, waiting for the war to begin, writes as follows:

"A Scotch soldier of fortune, Henry MacIver, a colonel by rank, has arrived at Belgrade with a small contingent of military adventurers. Five weeks ago I met him in Fleet Street, London, and had some talk about his 'expedition.' He had received a commission from the Prince of Servia to organize and command an independent cavalry brigade, and he then was busily enrolling his volunteers into a body styled 'The Knights of the Red Cross.' I am afraid some of his bold crusaders have earned more distinction for their attacks on Fleet Street bars than they are likely to earn on Servian battle-fields, but then I must not anticipate history."

Another paper tells that at the end of the first week of his service as a Servian officer, MacIver had enlisted ninety men, but that they were scattered about the town, many without shelter and rations:

"He assembled his men on the Rialto, and in spite of official expostulation, the men were marched up to the Minister's four abreast - and they marched fairly well, making a good show. The War Minister was taken by storm, and at once granted everything. It has raised the

English colonel's popularity with his men to fever heat."

This from the *Times*, London:

"Our Belgrade correspondent telegraphs last night:

"'There is here at present a gentleman named MacIver. He came from England to offer himself and his sword to the Servians. The Servian Minister of War gave him a colonel's commission. This morning I saw him drilling about one hundred and fifty remarkably fine-looking fellows, all clad in a good serviceable cavalry uniform, and he has horses.'"

Later we find that:

"Colonel MacIver's Legion of Cavalry, organizing here, now numbers over two hundred men."

And again:

"Prince Nica, a Roumanian cousin of the Princess Natalie of Servia, has joined Colonel MacIver's cavalry corps."

Later, in the *Court Journal*, October 28, 1876, we read:

"Colonel MacIver, who a few years ago was very well known in military circles in Dublin, now is making his mark with the Servian army. In the war against the Turks, he commands about one thousand Russo-Servian cavalry."

He was next to receive the following honors:

"Colonel MacIver has been appointed commander of the cavalry of the Servian armies on the Morava and Timok, and has received the Cross of the Takovo Order from General Tchemaieff for gallant conduct in the field, and the gold medal for valor."

Later we learn from the *Daily News*:

"Mr. Lewis Farley, Secretary of the 'League in Aid of Christians of Turkey,' has received the following letter, dated Belgrade, October 10, 1876:

"'DEAR SIR: In reference to the embroidered banner so kindly worked by an English lady and forwarded by the League to Colonel MacIver, I have great pleasure in conveying to you the following particulars. On Sunday morning, the flag having been previously consecrated by the archbishop, was conducted by a guard of honor to the palace, and Colonel MacIver, in the presence of Prince Milan and a numerous suite, in the name and on behalf of yourself and the fair donor, delivered it into the hands of the Princess Natalie. The gallant Colonel wore upon this occasion his full uniform as brigade commander and chief of cavalry of the Servian army, and bore upon his breast the 'Gold Cross of Takovo' which he received after the battles of the 28th and 30th of September, in recognition of the heroism and bravery he displayed upon these eventful days. The beauty of the decoration was enhanced by the circumstances of its bestowal, for on the evening of the battle of the 30th, General Tchernaieff approached Colonel MacIver, and, unclasping the cross from his own breast, placed it upon that of the Colonel.

"'(Signed.) HUGH JACKSON,
"'*Member of Council of the League*."

In Servia and in the Servian army MacIver reached what as yet is the highest point of his career, and of his life the happiest period.

He was *general de brigade*, which is not what we know as a brigade general, but is one who commands a division, a major-general. He was a great favorite both at the palace and with the people, the pay was good, fighting plentiful, and Belgrade gay and amusing. Of all the places he has visited and the countries he has served, it is of this Balkan kingdom that the general seems to speak most fondly and with the greatest feeling. Of Queen Natalie he was and is a most loyal and chivalric admirer, and was ever ready, when he found any one who did not as greatly respect the lady, to offer him the choice of swords or pistols. Even for Milan he finds an extenuating word.

After Servia the general raised more foreign legions, planned further expeditions; in Central America reorganized the small armies of the small republics, served as United States Consul, and offered his sword to President McKinley for use against Spain. But with Servia the most active portion of the life of the general ceased, and the rest has been a repetition of what went before. At present his time is divided between New York and Virginia, where he has been offered an executive position in the approaching Jamestown Exposition. Both North and South he has many friends, many admirers. But his life is, and, from the nature of his profession, must always be, a lonely one.

While other men remain planted in one spot, gathering about them a home, sons and daughters, an income for old age, MacIver is a rolling stone, a piece of floating sea-weed; as the present King of England called him fondly, "that vagabond soldier."

To a man who has lived in the saddle and upon transports, "neighbor" conveys nothing, and even "comrade" too often means one who is no longer living.

With the exception of the United States, of which he now is a naturalized citizen, the general has fought for nearly every country in the world, but if any of those for which he lost his health and blood, and for which he risked his life, remembers him, it makes no sign. And the general is too proud to ask to be remembered. To-day there is no more interesting figure than this man who in years is still young enough to lead an army corps, and who, for forty years, has been selling his sword and risking his life for presidents, pretenders, charlatans, and emperors.

He finds some mighty changes: Cuba, which he fought to free, is free; men of the South, with whom for four years he fought shoulder to shoulder, are now wearing the blue; the empire of Mexico, for which he fought, is a republic; the empire of France, for which he fought, is a republic; the empire of Brazil, for which he fought is a republic; the dynasty in Servia, to which he owes his greatest honors, has been wiped out by murder. From none of the eighteen countries he has served has he a pension, berth, or billet, and at sixty he finds himself at home in every land, but with a home in none.

Still he has his sword, his blanket, and in the event of war, to obtain a commission he has only to open his tin boxes and show the commissions already won. Indeed, any day, in a new uniform, and under the Nineteenth

Flag, the general may again be winning fresh victories and honors.

And so, this brief sketch of him is left unfinished. We will mark it - *To be continued.*

BARON JAMES HARDEN-HICKEY

THIS is an attempt to tell the story of Baron Harden-Hickey, the Man Who Made Himself King, the man who was born after his time.

If the reader, knowing something of the strange career of Harden-Hickey, wonders why one writes of him appreciatively rather than in amusement, he is asked not to judge Harden-Hickey as one judges a contemporary.

Harden-Hickey, in our day, was as incongruous a figure as was the American at the Court of King Arthur; he was as unhappily out of the picture as would be Cyrano de Bergerac on the floor of the Board of Trade. Judged, as at the time he was judged, by writers of comic paragraphs, by presidents of railroads, by amateur "statesmen" at Washington, Harden-Hickey was a joke. To the vacant mind of the village idiot, Rip Van Winkle returning to Falling Water also was a joke. The people of our day had not the time to understand Harden-Hickey; they thought him a charlatan, half a dangerous adventurer and half a fool; and Harden-Hickey certainly did not under stand them. His last words, addressed to his wife, showed this. They were: "I would rather die a gentleman than live a blackguard like your father."

As a matter of fact, his father-in-law, although living under the disadvantage of being a Standard Oil magnate, neither was, nor is, a blackguard, and his son-in-law had been treated by him generously and with patience. But for the duellist and soldier of fortune it was impossible to sympathize with a man who took no greater risk in life than to ride on one of his own railroads, and of the views the two men held of each other, that of John H. Flagler was probably the fairer and the more kindly.

Harden-Hickey was one of the most picturesque, gallant, and pathetic adventurers of our day; but Flagler also deserves our sympathy.

For an unimaginative and hard-working Standard Oil king to have a D'Artagnan thrust upon him as a son-in-law must be trying.

James A. Harden-Hickey, James the First of Trinidad, Baron of the Holy Roman Empire, was born on December 8, 1854. As to the date all historians agree; as to where the important event took place they differ. That he was born in France his friends are positive, but at the time of his death in El Paso the San Francisco papers claimed him as a native of California. All agree that his ancestors were Catholics and Royalists who left Ireland with the Stuarts when they sought refuge in France. The version which seems to be the most probable is that he was born in San Francisco, where as one of the early settlers, his father, E. C. Hickey, was well known, and that early in his life, in order to educate him, the mother took him to Europe.

There he was educated at the Jesuit College at Namur, then at Leipsic, and later entered the Military College of St. Cyr.

James the First was one of those boys who never had the misfortune to grow up. To the moment of his death, in all he planned you can trace the effects of his early teachings and environment; the influences of the great Church that nursed him, and of the city of Paris, in which he lived. Under the Second Empire, Paris was at her maddest, baddest, and best. To-day under the republic, without a court, with a society kept in funds by the self-expatriated wives and daughters of our business men, she lacks the reasons for which Baron Haussmann bedecked her and made her beautiful. The good Loubet, the worthy Fallieres, except that they furnish the cartoonist with subjects for ridicule, do not add to the gayety of Paris. But when Harden-Hickey was a boy, Paris was never so carelessly gay, so brilliant, never so overcharged with life, color, and adventure.

In those days "the Emperor sat in his box that night," and in the box opposite sat Cora Pearl; veterans of the campaign of Italy, of Mexico, from the desert fights of Algiers, sipped sugar and water in front of Tortoni's, the Cafe Durand, the Cafe Riche; the sidewalks rang with their sabres, the boulevards were filled with the colors of the gorgeous uniforms; all night of each night the Place Vendome shone with the carriage lamps of the visiting pashas from Egypt, of nabobs from India, of *rastaquoueres* from the sister empire of Brazil; the state carriages, with the outriders and postilions in the green and gold of the Empress, swept through the Champs Elysees, and at the Bal Bulier, and at Mabile the students and "grisettes" introduced the cancan. The men of those days were Hugo, Thiers, Dumas, Daudet, Alfred de Musset; the magnificent blackguard, the Duc de Morny, and the great, simple Canrobert, the captain of barricades, who became a marshal of France.

Over all was the mushroom Emperor, his anterooms crowded with the titled charlatans of Europe, his court radiant with countesses created overnight. And it was the Emperor, with his love of theatrical display, of gorgeous ceremonies; with his restless reaching after military glory, the weary, cynical adventurer, that the boy at St. Cyr took as his model.

Royalist as was Harden-Hickey by birth and tradition, and Royalist as he always remained, it was the court at the Tuileries that filled his imagination. The Bourbons, whom he served, hoped some day for a court; at the Tuileries there was a court, glittering before his physical eyes. The Bourbons were pleasant old gentlemen, who later willingly supported him, and for whom always he was equally willing to fight, either with his sword or his pen. But to the last, in his mind, he carried pictures of the Second Empire as he, as a boy, had known it.

Can you not imagine the future James the First, barelegged, in a black-belted smock, halting with his nurse, or his priest, to gaze up in awestruck delight at the great, red-breeched Zouaves lounging on guard at the Tuileries?

"When I grow up," said little James to himself, not knowing that he never would grow up, "I shall have Zouaves for *my* palace guard."

And twenty years later, when he laid down the laws for his little kingdom, you find that the officers of his court must wear the mustache, "*a la* Louis Napoleon," and that the Zouave uniform will be worn by the Palace Guards.

In 1883, while he still was at the War College, his father died, and when he graduated, which he did with honors, he found himself his own master. His assets were a small income, a perfect knowledge of the French language, and the reputation of being one of the most expert swordsman in Paris. He chose not to enter the army, and instead became a journalist, novelist, duellist, an *habitue* of the Latin Quarter and the boulevards.

As a novelist the titles of his books suggest their quality. Among them are: "Un Amour Vendeen," "Lettres d'un Yankee," "Un Amour dans le Monde," "Memoires d'un Gommeux," "Merveilleuses Aventures de Nabuchodonosor, Nosebreaker."

Of the Catholic Church he wrote seriously, apparently with deep conviction, with high enthusiasm. In her service as a defender of the faith he issued essays, pamphlets, "broadsides." The opponents of the Church in Paris he attacked relentlessly.

As a reward for his championship he received the title of baron.

In 1878, while only twenty-four, he married the Countess de Saint-Pery, by whom he had two children, a boy and a girl, and three years later he started *Triboulet*. It was this paper that made him famous to "all Paris."

It was a Royalist sheet, subsidized by the Count de Chambord and published in the interest of the

Bourbons. Until 1888 Harden-Hickey was its editor, and even by his enemies it must be said that he served his employers with zeal. During the seven years in which the paper amused Paris and annoyed the republican government, as its editor Harden-Hickey was involved in forty-two lawsuits, for different editorial indiscretions, fined three hundred thousand francs, and was a principal in countless duels.

To his brother editors his standing interrogation was: "Would you prefer to meet me upon the editorial page, or in the Bois de Boulogne?" Among those who met him in the Bois were Aurelien Scholl, H. Lavenbryon, M. Taine, M. de Cyon, Philippe Du Bois, Jean Moreas.

In 1888, either because, his patron the Count de Chambord having died, there was no more money to pay the fines, or because the patience of the government was exhausted, *Triboulet* ceased to exist, and Harden-Hickey, claiming the paper had been suppressed and he himself exiled, crossed to London.

From there he embarked upon a voyage around the world, which lasted two years, and in the course of which he discovered the island kingdom of which he was to be the first and last king. Previous to his departure, having been divorced from the Countess de Saint-Pery, he placed his boy and girl in the care of a fellow-journalist and very dear friend, the Count de la Boissiere, of whom later we shall hear more.

Harden-Hickey started around the world on the *Astoria*, a British merchant vessel bound for India by way of Cape Horn, Captain Jackson commanding.

When off the coast of Brazil the ship touched at the

uninhabited island of Trinidad. Historians of James the First say that it was through stress of weather that the *Astoria* was driven to seek refuge there, but as, for six months of the year, to make a landing on the island is almost impossible, and as at any time, under stress of weather, Trinidad would be a place to avoid, it is more likely Jackson put in to replenish his water-casks, or to obtain a supply of turtle meat.

Or it may have been that, having told Harden-Hickey of the derelict island, the latter persuaded the captain to allow him to land and explore it. Of this, at least, we are certain, a boat was sent ashore, Harden-Hickey went ashore in it, and before he left the island, as a piece of no man's land, belonging to no country, he claimed it in his own name, and upon the beach raised a flag of his own design.

The island of Trinidad claimed by Harden-Hickey must not be confused with the larger Trinidad belonging to Great Britain and lying off Venezuela.

The English Trinidad is a smiling, peaceful spot of great tropical beauty; it is one of the fairest places in the West Indies. At every hour of the year the harbor of Port of Spain holds open its arms to vessels of every draught. A governor in a pith helmet, a cricket club, a bishop in gaiters, and a botanical garden go to make it a prosperous and contented colony. But the little derelict Trinidad, in latitude 20 degrees 30 minutes south, and longitude 29 degrees 22 minutes west, seven hundred miles from the coast of Brazil, is but a spot upon the ocean. On most maps it is not even a spot. Except by birds, turtles, and hideous land-crabs, it is uninhabited; and against the advances of man its shores are fortified with cruel ridges of coral, jagged limestone rocks, and a tremendous towering surf which, even in a dead calm, beats many feet high against the coast.

In 1698 Dr. Halley visited the island, and says he found nothing living but doves and land-crabs. "Saw many green turtles in sea, but by reason of the great surf, could catch none."

After Halley's visit, in 1700 the island was settled by a few Portuguese from Brazil. The ruins of their stone huts are still in evidence. But Amaro Delano, who called in 1803, makes no mention of the Portuguese; and when, in 1822, Commodore Owen visited Trinidad, he found nothing living there save cormorants, petrels, gannets, man-of-war birds, and "turtles weighing from five hundred to seven hundred pounds."

In 1889 E. F. Knight, who in the Japanese-Russian War represented the London *Morning Post*, visited Trinidad in his yacht in search of buried treasure.

Alexander Dalrymple, in his book entitled "Collection of Voages, chiefly in the Southern Atlantick Ocean, 1775," tells how, in 1700, he "took possession of the island in his Majesty's name as knowing it to be granted by the King's letter patent, leaving a Union Jack flying."

So it appears that before Harden-Hickey seized the island it already had been claimed by Great Britain, and later, on account of the Portuguese settlement, by Brazil. The answer Harden-Hickey made to these claims was that the English never settled in Trinidad, and that the Portuguese abandoned it, and, therefore, their claims lapsed. In his "prospectus" of his island, Harden-Hickey himself describes it thus:

"Trinidad is about five miles long and three miles wide. In spite of its rugged and uninviting appearance, the inland plateaus are rich with luxuriant vegetation.

"Prominent among this is a peculiar species of bean, which is not only edible, but extremely palatable. The surrounding seas swarm with fish, which as yet are wholly unsuspicious of the hook. Dolphins, rock-cod, pigfish, and blackfish may be caught as quickly as they can be hauled out. I look to the sea birds and the turtles to afford our principal source of revenue. Trinidad is the breeding-place of almost the entire feathery population of the South Atlantic Ocean. The exportation of guano alone should make my little country prosperous. Turtles visit the island to deposit eggs, and at certain seasons the beach is literally alive with them. The only drawback to my projected kingdom is the fact that it has no good harbor and can be approached only when the sea is calm."

As a matter of fact sometimes months pass before it is possible to effect a landing.

Another asset of the island held out by the prospectus was its great store of buried treasure. Before Harden-Hickey seized the island, this treasure had made it known. This is the legend. In 1821 a great store of gold and silver plate plundered from Peruvian churches had been concealed on the islands by pirates near Sugar Loaf Hill, on the shore of what is known as the Southwest Bay. Much of this plate came from the cathedral at Lima, having been carried from there during the war of independence when the Spanish residents fled the country. In their eagerness to escape they put to sea in any ship that offered, and these unarmed and unseaworthy vessels fell an easy prey to pirates. One of these pirates on his death-bed, in gratitude to his former captain, told him the secret of the treasure. In 1892 this captain was still living, in Newcastle, England, and although his story bears a family resemblance to every other story of buried treasure, there were added to the tale of the pirate some corroborative details. These, in twelve years, induced five different expeditions to visit the island. The two most important were that of E. F. Knight and one from the Tyne in the bark *Aurea*.

In his "Cruise of the *Alerte*," Knight gives a full description of the island, and of his attempt to find the treasure. In this, a landslide having covered the place where it was buried, he was unsuccessful.

But Knight's book is the only source of accurate information concerning Trinidad, and in writing his prospectus it is evident that Harden-Hickey was forced to borrow from it freely. Knight himself says that the most minute and accurate description of Trinidad is to be found in the "Frank Mildmay" of Captain Marryat. He found it so easy to identify each spot mentioned in the novel that he believes the author of "Midshipman Easy" himself touched there.

After seizing Trinidad, Harden-Hickey rounded the Cape and made north to Japan, China, and India. In India he became interested in Buddhism, and remained for over a year questioning the priests of that religion and studying its tenets and history.

On his return to Paris, in 1890, he met Miss Annie Harper Flagler, daughter of John H. Flagler. A year later, on St. Patrick's Day, 1891, at the Fifth Avenue Presbyterian Church, Miss Flagler became the Baroness Harden-Hickey. The Rev. John Hall married them.

For the next two years Harden-Hickey lived in New York, but so quietly that, except that he lived quietly, it is difficult to find out anything concerning him. The man who, a few years before, had delighted Paris with his daily feuilletons, with his duels, with his forty-two lawsuits, who had been the master of revels in the Latin Quarter, in New York lived almost as a recluse, writing a book on Buddhism. While he was in New York I was a reporter on the *Evening Sun*, but I cannot recall ever having read his name in the newspapers of that day, and I heard of him only twice; once as giving an exhibition of his water-colors at the American Art Galleries, and again as the author of a book I found in a store in Twenty-second Street, just east of Broadway, then the home of the Truth Seeker Publishing Company.

It was a grewsome compilation and had just appeared in print. It was called "Euthanasia, or the Ethics of Suicide." This book was an apology or plea for self-destruction. In it the baron laid down those occasions when he considered suicide pardonable, and when obligatory. To support his arguments and to show that suicide was a noble act, he quoted Plato, Cicero, Shakespeare, and even misquoted the Bible. He gave a list of poisons, and the amount of each necessary to kill a human being. To show how one can depart from life with the least pain, he illustrated the text with most unpleasant pictures, drawn by himself.

The book showed how far Harden-Hickey had strayed from the teachings of the Jesuit College at Namur, and of the Church that had made him "noble."

All of these two years had not been spent only in New York. Harden-Hickey made excursions to California, to Mexico, and to Texas, and in each of these places bought cattle ranches and mines. The money to pay for these investments came from his father-in-law. But not directly. Whenever he wanted money he asked his wife, or De la Boissiere, who was a friend also of Flagler, to obtain it for him.

His attitude toward his father-in-law is difficult to explain. It is not apparent that Flagler ever did anything which could justly offend him; indeed, he always seems to have spoken of his son-in-law with tolerance, and often with awe, as one would speak of a clever, wayward child. But Harden-Hickey chose to regard Flagler as his enemy, as a sordid man of business who could not understand the feelings and aspirations of a genius and a gentleman.

Before Harden-Hickey married, the misunderstanding between his wife's father and himself began. Because he thought Harden-Hickey was marrying his daughter for her money, Flagler opposed the union. Consequently, Harden-Hickey married Miss Flagler without "settlements," and for the first few years supported her without aid from her father. But his wife had been accustomed to a manner of living beyond the means of the soldier of fortune, and soon his income, and then even his capital, was exhausted. From her mother the baroness inherited a fortune. This was in the hands of her father as executor. When his own money was gone, Harden-Hickey endeavored to have the money belonging to his wife placed to her credit, or to his. To this, it is said, Flagler, on the ground that Harden-Hickey was not a man of business, while he was, objected, and urged that he was, and that if it remained in his hands the money would be better invested and better expended. It was the refusal of Flagler to intrust Harden-Hickey with the care of his wife's money that caused the breach between them.

As I have said, you cannot judge Harden-Hickey as you would a contemporary. With the people among whom he was thrown, his ideas were entirely out of joint. He should have lived in the days of "The Three Musketeers." People who looked upon him as working for his own hand entirely misunderstood him. He was absolutely honest, and as absolutely without a sense of humor. To him, to pay taxes, to pay grocers' bills, to depend for protection upon a policeman, was intolerable. He lived in a world of his own imagining. And one day, in order to make his imaginings real, and to escape from his father-in-law's unromantic world of Standard Oil and Florida hotels, in a proclamation to the powers he announced himself as King James the First of the Principality of Trinidad.

The proclamation failed to create a world crisis. Several of the powers recognized his principality and his title; but, as a rule, people laughed, wondered, and forgot. That the daughter of John Flagler was to rule the new principality gave it a "news interest," and for a few Sundays in the supplements she was hailed as the "American Queen."

When upon the subject of the new kingdom Flagler himself was interviewed, he showed an open mind.

"My son-in-law is a very determined man," he said; "he will carry out any scheme in which he is interested. Had he consulted me about this, I would have been glad to have aided him with money or advice. My son-in-law is an extremely well-read, refined, well-bred man. He does not court publicity. While he was staying in my house he spent nearly all the time in the library translating an Indian book on Buddhism. My daughter has no ambition to be a queen or anything else than what she is - an American girl. But my son-in-law means to carry on this Trinidad scheme, and - he will."

From his father-in-law, at least, Harden-Hickey could not complain that he had met with lack of sympathy.

The rest of America was amused; and after less than nine days, indifferent. But Harden-Hickey, though unobtrusively, none the less earnestly continued to play the part of king. His friend De la Boissiere he appointed his Minister of Foreign Affairs, and established in a Chancellery at 217 West Thirty-sixth Street, New York, and from there was issued a sort of circular, or prospectus, written by the king, and signed by "Le Grand Chancelier, Secretaire d'Etat pour les Affaires Etrangeres, M. le Comte de la Boissiere."

The document, written in French, announced that the new state would be governed by a military dictatorship, that the royal standard was a yellow triangle on a red ground, and that the arms of the principality were "d'Or chape de Gueules." It pointed out naively that those who first settled on the island would be naturally the oldest inhabitants, and hence would form the aristocracy. But only those who at home enjoyed social position and some private fortune would be admitted into this select circle.

For itself the state reserved a monopoly of the guano, of the turtles, and of the buried treasure. And both to discover the treasure and to encourage settlers to dig and so cultivate the soil, a percentage of the treasure was promised to the one who found it.

Any one purchasing ten $200 bonds was entitled to a free passage to the island, and after a year, should he so desire it, a return trip. The hard work was to be performed by Chinese coolies, the aristocracy existing beautifully, and, according to the prospectus, to enjoy *"vie d'un genre tout nouveau, et la recherche de sensations nouvelles."*

To reward his subjects for prominence in literature, the arts, and the sciences, his Majesty established an order of chivalry. The official document creating this order reads:

"We, James, Prince of Trinidad, have resolved to commemorate our accession to the throne of Trinidad by the institution of an Order of Chivalry, destined to reward literature, industry, science, and the human virtues, and by these presents have established and do institute, with cross and crown, the Order of the Insignia of the Cross of Trinidad, of which we and our heirs and successors shall be the sovereigns.

"Given in our Chancellery the Eighth of the month of December, one thousand eight hundred and ninety-three, and of our reign, the First Year.

"JAMES."

There were four grades: Chevalier, Commander, Grand Officer, and Grand Cross; and the name of each member of the order was inscribed in "The Book of Gold." A pension of one thousand francs was given to a Chevalier, of two thousand francs to a Commander, and of three thousand francs to a Grand Officer. Those of the grade of Grand Cross were content with a plaque of eight diamond-studded rays, with, in the centre, set in red enamel, the arms of Trinidad. The ribbon was red and yellow.

A rule of the order read: "The costume shall be identical with that of the Chamberlains of the Court of Trinidad, save the buttons, which shall bear the impress of the Crown of the Order."

For himself, King James commissioned a firm of jewelers to construct a royal crown. In design it was similar to the one which surmounted the cross of Trinidad. It is shown in the photograph of the insignia. Also, the king issued a set of postage-stamps on which was a picture of the island. They were of various colors and denominations, and among stamp-collectors enjoyed a certain sale.

To-day, as I found when I tried to procure one to use in this book, they are worth many times their face value.

For some time the affairs of the new kingdom progressed favorably. In San Francisco, King James, in person, engaged four hundred coolies and fitted out a schooner which he sent to Trinidad, where it made regular trips between his principality and Brazil; an agent was established on the island, and the construction of docks, wharves, and houses was begun, while at the chancellery in West Thirty-sixth Street, the

Minister of Foreign Affairs was ready to furnish would-be settlers with information.

And then, out of a smiling sky, a sudden and unexpected blow was struck at the independence of the little kingdom. It was a blow from which it never recovered.

In July of 1895, while constructing a cable to Brazil, Great Britain found the Island of Trinidad lying in the direct line she wished to follow, and, as a cable station, seized it. Objection to this was made by Brazil, and at Bahia a mob with stones pelted the sign of the English Consul-General.

By right of Halley's discovery, England claimed the island; as a derelict from the main land, Brazil also claimed it. Between the rivals, the world saw a chance for war, and the fact that the island really belonged to our King James for a moment was forgotten.

But the Minister of Foreign Affairs was at his post. With promptitude and vigor he acted. He addressed a circular note to all the powers of Europe, and to our State Department a protest. It read as follows:

"GRANDE CHANCELLERIE DE LA
PRINCIPAUTE DE
TRINIDAD,
27 WEST THIRTY-SIXTH STREET,
NEW YORK CITY, U. S. A.,

"NEW YORK, *July* 30, 1895.

"To His Excellency Mr. the Secretary of State of the Republic of the United States of North America, Washington, D. C.:

"EXCELLENCY. - I have the honor to recall to your memory:

"1. That in the course of the month of September, 1893, Baron Harden-Hickey officially notified all the Powers of his taking possession of the uninhabited island of Trinidad; and

"2. That in course of January, 1894, he renewed to all these Powers the official notification of the said taking of possession, and informed them at the same time that from that date the land would be known as 'Principality of Trinidad'; that he took the title of 'Prince of Trinidad,' and would reign under the name of James I.

"In consequence of these official notifications several Powers have recognized the new Principality and its Prince, and at all events none thought it necessary at that epoch to raise objections or formulate opposition.

"The press of the entire world has, on the other hand, often acquainted readers with these facts, thus giving to them all possible publicity. In consequence of the accomplishment of these various formalities, and as the law of nations prescribes that 'derelict' territories belong to whoever will take possession of them, and as the island of Trinidad, which has been abandoned for years, certainly belongs to the aforesaid category, his Serene Highness Prince James I was authorized to regard his rights on the said island as perfectly valid and indisputable.

"Nevertheless, your Excellency knows that recently, in spite of all the legitimate rights of my august sovereign, an English war-ship has disembarked at Trinidad a detachment of armed troops and taken possession of the island in the name of England.

"Following this assumption of territory, the Brazilian Government, invoking a right of ancient Portuguese occupation (long ago outlawed), has notified the English Government to surrender the island to Brazil.

"I beg of your Excellency to ask of the Government of the United States of North America to recognize the Principality of Trinidad as an independent State, and to come to an understanding with the other American Powers in order to guarantee its neutrality.

"Thus the Government of the United States of North America will once more accord its powerful assistance to the cause of right and of justice, misunderstood by England and Brazil, put an end to a situation which threatens to disturb the peace, re-establish concord between two great States ready to appeal to arms, and affirm itself, moreover, as the faithful interpreter of the Monroe Doctrine.

"In the expectation of your reply please accept, Excellency, the expression of my elevated consideration.

"The Grand Chancellor, Secretary for Foreign Affairs,

"COMTE DE LA BOISSIERE."

At that time Richard Olney was Secretary of State, and in his treatment of the protest, and of the gentleman who wrote it, he fully upheld the reputation he made while in office of lack of good manners. Saying he was unable to read the handwriting in which the protest was written, he disposed of it in a way that would suggest itself naturally to a statesman and a gentleman. As a "crank" letter he turned it over to the Washington correspondents. You can imagine what they did with it.

The day following the reporters in New York swept down upon the chancellery and upon the Minister of Foreign Affairs. It was the "silly season" in August, there was no real news in town, and the troubles of De la Boissiere were allowed much space.

They laughed at him and at his king, at his chancellery, at his broken English, at his "grave and courtly manners," even at his clothes. But in spite of the ridicule, between the lines you could read that to the man himself it all was terribly real.

I had first heard of the island of Trinidad from two men I knew who spent three months on it searching for the treasure, and when Harden-Hickey proclaimed himself lord of the island, through the papers I had carefully followed his fortunes. So, partly out of curiosity and partly out of sympathy, I called at the chancellery.

I found it in a brownstone house, in a dirty neighborhood just west of Seventh Avenue, and of where now stands the York Hotel. Three weeks ago I revisited it and found it unchanged. At the time of my first visit, on the jamb of the front door was pasted a piece of paper on which was written in the handwriting of De la Boissiere: "Chancellerie de la Principaute de Trinidad."

The chancellery was not exactly in its proper setting. On its door-step children of the tenements were playing dolls with clothes-pins; in the street a huckster in raucous tones was offering wilted cabbages to women in wrappers leaning from the fire escapes; the smells and the heat of New York in midsummer rose from the asphalt. It was a far cry to the wave-swept island off the coast of Brazil.

De la Boissiere received me with distrust. The morning papers had made him man-shy; but, after a few "Your Excellencies" and a respectful inquiry regarding "His Royal Highness," his confidence revived. In the situation he saw nothing humorous, not even in an announcement on the wall which read: "Sailings to Trinidad." Of these there were *two*; on March 1, and on October 1. On the table were many copies of the royal proclamation, the postage-stamps of the new government, the thousand-franc bonds, and, in pasteboard boxes, the gold and red enamelled crosses of the Order of Trinidad.

He talked to me frankly and fondly of Prince James. Indeed, I never met any man who knew Harden-Hickey well who did not speak of him with aggressive loyalty. If at his eccentricities they smiled, it was with the smile of affection. It was easy to see De la Boissiere regarded him not only with the affection of a friend, but with the devotion of a true subject. In his manner he himself was courteous, gentle, and so distinguished that I felt as though I were enjoying, on intimate terms, an audience with one of the prime-ministers of Europe.

And he, on his part, after the ridicule of the morning papers, to have any one with outward seriousness accept his high office and his king, was, I believe, not ungrateful.

I told him I wished to visit Trinidad, and in that I was quite serious. The story of an island filled with buried treasure, and governed by a king, whose native subjects were turtles and seagulls, promised to make interesting writing.

The count was greatly pleased. I believe in me he saw his first bona-fide settler, and when I rose to go he even lifted one of the crosses of Trinidad and, before my envious eyes, regarded it uncertainly.

Perhaps, had he known that of all decorations it was the one I most desired; had I only then and there booked my passage, or sworn allegiance to King James, who knows but that to-day I might be a chevalier, with my name in the "Book of Gold"? But instead of bending the knee, I reached for my hat; the count replaced the cross in its pasteboard box, and for me the psychological moment had passed.

Others, more deserving of the honor, were more fortunate. Among my fellow-reporters who, like myself, came to scoff, and remained to pray, was Henri Pene du Bois, for some time, until his recent death, the brilliant critic of art and music of the *American*. Then he was on the *Times*, and Henry N. Cary, now of the *Morning Telegraph*, was his managing editor.

When Du Bois reported to Cary on his assignment, he said: "There is nothing funny in that story. It's pathetic. Both those men are in earnest. They are convinced they are being robbed of their rights. Their only fault is that they have imagination, and that the rest of us lack it. That's the way it struck me, and that's the way the story ought to be written."

"Write it that way," said Cary.

So, of all the New York papers, the *Times*, for a brief period, became the official organ of the Government of James the First, and in time Cary and Du Bois were created Chevaliers of the Order of Trinidad, and entitled to wear uniforms "Similar to those of the Chamberlains of the Court, save that the buttons bear the impress of the Royal Crown."

The attack made by Great Britain and Brazil upon the independence of the principality, while it left Harden-Hickey in the position of a king in exile, brought him at once another crown, which, by those who offered it to him, was described as of incomparably greater value than that of Trinidad.

In the first instance the man had sought the throne; in this case the throne sought the man.

In 1893 in San Francisco, Ralston J. Markowe, a lawyer and a one-time officer of artillery in the United States army, gained renown as one of the Morrow filibustering expedition which attempted to overthrow the Dole government in the Hawaiian Isles and restore to the throne Queen Liliuokalani. In San Francisco Markowe was nicknamed the "Prince of Honolulu," as it was understood, should Liliuokalani regain her crown, he would be rewarded with some high office. But in the star of Liliuokalani, Markowe apparently lost faith, and thought he saw in Harden-Hickey timber more suitable for king-making. Accordingly, twenty-four days after the "protest" was sent to our State

Department, Markowe switched his allegiance to Harden-Hickey, and to him addressed the following letter:

"SAN FRANCISCO, August 26, 1895.

BARON HARDEN-HICKEY, LOS ANGELES, CAL.:

"Monseigneur - Your favor of August 16 has been received.

"1. I am the duly authorized agent of the Royalist party in so far as it is possible for any one to occupy that position under existing circumstances. With the Queen in prison and absolutely cut off from all communication with her friends, it is out of the question for me to carry anything like formal credentials.

"2. Alienating any part of the territory cannot give rise to any constitutional questions, for the reason that the constitutions, like the land tenures, are in a state of such utter confusion that only a strong hand can unravel them, and the restoration will result in the establishment of a strong military government. If I go down with the expedition I have organized I shall be in full control of the situation and in a position to carry out all my contracts.

"3. It is the island of Kauai on which I propose to establish you as an independent sovereign.

"4. My plan is to successively occupy all the islands, leaving the capital to the last. When the others have fallen, the capital, being cut off from all its resources, will be easily taken, and may very likely fall without effort. I don't expect in any case to have to fortify myself or to take the defensive, or to have to issue a call to arms, as I shall have an overwhelming force to join me at once, in addition to those who go with me, who by themselves will be sufficient to carry everything before them without active cooperation from the people there.

"5. The Government forces consist of about 160 men and boys, with very imperfect military training, and of whom about forty are officers. They are organized as infantry. There are also about 600 citizens enrolled as a reserve guard, who may be called upon in case of an emergency, and about 150 police. We can fully rely upon the assistance of all the police and from one-quarter to one-half of the other troops. And of the remainder many will under no circumstances engage in a sharp fight in defense of the present government. There are now on the island plenty of men and arms to accomplish our purpose, and if my expedition does not get off very soon the people there will be organized to do the work without other assistance from here than the direction of a few leaders, of which they stand more in need than anything else.

"6. The tonnage of the vessel is 146. She at present has berth-room for twenty men, but bunks can be arranged in the hold for 256 more, with provision for ample ventilation. She has one complete set of sails and two extra spars. The remaining information in regard to her I will have to obtain and send you to-morrow. I think it must be clear to you that the opportunity now offered you will be of incomparably greater value at once than Trinidad would ever be. Still hoping that I may have an interview with you at an early date, respectfully yours,

"RALSTON J. MARKOWE."

What Harden-Hickey thought of this is not known, but as two weeks before he received it he had written Markowe, asking him by what authority he represented the Royalists of Honolulu, it seems evident that when the crown of Hawaii was first proffered him he did not at once spurn it.

He now was in the peculiar position of being a deposed king of an island in the South Atlantic, which had been taken from him, and king-elect of an island in the Pacific, which was his if he could take it.

This was in August of 1895. For the two years following, Harden-Hickey was a soldier of misfortunes. Having lost his island kingdom, he could no longer occupy himself with plans for its improvement. It had been his toy. They had taken it from him, and the loss and the ridicule which followed hurt him bitterly.

And for the lands he really owned in Mexico and California, and which, if he were to live in comfort, it was necessary he should sell, he could find no purchaser; and, moreover, having quarrelled with his father-in-law, he had cut off his former supply of money. The need of it pinched him cruelly.

The advertised cause of this quarrel was sufficiently characteristic to be the real one. Moved by the attack of Great Britain upon his principality, Harden-Hickey decided upon reprisals. It must be remembered that always he was more Irish than French. On paper he organized an invasion of England from Ireland, the home of his ancestors. It was because Flagler refused to give him money for this adventure that he broke with him. His friends say this was the real reason of the quarrel, which was a quarrel on the side of Harden-Hickey alone.

And there were other, more intimate troubles. While not separated from his wife, he now was seldom in her company. When the Baroness was in Paris, Harden-Hickey was in San Francisco; when she returned to San Francisco, he was in Mexico. The fault seems to have been his. He was greatly admired by pretty women. His daughter by his first wife, now a very beautiful girl of sixteen, spent much time with her stepmother; and when not on his father's ranch in Mexico, his son also, for months together, was at her side. The husband approved of this, but he himself saw his wife infrequently. Nevertheless, early in the spring of 1898, the Baroness leased a house in Brockton Square, in Riverside, Cal., where it was understood by herself and by her friends her husband would join her. At that time in Mexico he was trying to dispose of a large tract of land. Had he been able to sell it, the money for a time would have kept one even of his extravagances contentedly rich. At least, he would have been independent of his wife and of her father. Up to February of 1898 his obtaining this money seemed probable.

Early in that month the last prospective purchaser decided not to buy.

There is no doubt that had Harden-Hickey then turned to his father-in-law, that gentleman, as he had done before, would have opened an account for him.

But the Prince of Trinidad felt he could no longer beg,

even for the money belonging to his wife, from the man he had insulted. He could no longer ask his wife to intercede for him. He was without money of his own, with out the means of obtaining it; from his wife he had ceased to expect even sympathy, and from the world he knew, the fact that he was a self-made king caused him always to be pointed out with ridicule as a charlatan, as a jest.

The soldier of varying fortunes, the duellist and dreamer, the devout Catholic and devout Buddhist, saw the forty-third year of his life only as the meeting-place of many fiascos.

His mind was tormented with imaginary wrongs, imaginary slights, imaginary failures.

This young man, who could paint pictures, write books, organize colonies oversea, and with a sword pick the buttons from a waistcoat, forgot the twenty good years still before him; forgot that men loved him for the mistakes he had made; that in parts of the great city of Paris his name was still spoken fondly, still was famous and familiar.

In his book on the "Ethics of Suicide," for certain hard places in life he had laid down an inevitable rule of conduct.

As he saw it he had come to one of those hard places, and he would not ask of others what he himself would not perform.

From Mexico he set out for California, but not to the house his wife had prepared for him.

Instead, on February 9, 1898, at El Paso, he left the train and registered at a hotel.

At 7.30 in the evening he went to his room, and when, on the following morning, they kicked in the door, they found him stretched rigidly upon the bed, like one lying in state, with, near his hand, a half-emptied bottle of poison.

On a chair was pinned this letter to his wife:

"My DEAREST, - No news from you, although you have had plenty of time to write. Harvey has written me that he has no one in view at present to buy my land. Well, I shall have tasted the cup of bitterness to the very dregs, but I do not complain. Good-by. I forgive you your conduct toward me and trust you will be able to forgive yourself. I prefer to be a dead gentleman to a living blackguard like your father."

And when they searched his open trunk for something that might identify the body on the bed, they found the crown of Trinidad.

You can imagine it: the mean hotel bedroom, the military figure with its white face and mustache, "*a la* Louis Napoleon," at rest upon the pillow, the startled drummers and chambermaids peering in from the hall, and the landlord, or coroner, or doctor, with a bewildered countenance, lifting to view the royal crown of gilt and velvet.

The other actors in this, as Harold Frederic called it, "Opera Bouffe Monarchy," are still living.

The Baroness Harden-Hickey makes her home in

this country.

The Count de la Boissiere, ex-Minister of Foreign Affairs, is still a leader of the French colony in New York, and a prosperous commission merchant with a suite of offices on Fifty-fourth Street. By the will of Harden-Hickey he is executor of his estate, guardian of his children, and what, for the purpose of this article, is of more importance, in his hands lies the future of the kingdom of Trinidad. When Harden-Hickey killed himself the title to the island was in dispute. Should young Harden-Hickey wish to claim it, it still would be in dispute. Meanwhile, by the will of the First James, De la Boissiere is appointed perpetual regent, a sort of "receiver," and executor of the principality.

To him has been left a royal decree signed and sealed, but blank. In the will the power to fill in this blank with a statement showing the final disposition of the island has been bestowed upon De la Boissiere.

So, some day, he may proclaim the accession of a new king, and give a new lease of life to the kingdom of which Harden-Hickey dreamed.

But unless his son, or wife, or daughter should assert his or her rights, which is not likely to happen, so ends the dynasty of James the First of Trinidad, Baron of the Holy Roman Empire.

To the wise ones in America he was a fool, and they laughed at him; to the wiser ones, he was a clever rascal who had evolved a new real-estate scheme and was out to rob the people - and they respected him. To my mind, of them all, Harden-Hickey was the wisest.

Granted one could be serious, what could be more delightful than to be your own king on your own island?

The comic paragraphers, the business men of "hard, common sense," the captains of industry who laughed at him and his national resources of buried treasure, turtles' eggs, and guano, with his body-guard of Zouaves and his Grand Cross of Trinidad, certainly possessed many things that Harden-Hickey lacked. But they in turn lacked the things that made him happy; the power to "make believe," the love of romance, the touch of adventure that plucked him by the sleeve.

When, as boys, we used to say: "Let's pretend we're pirates," as a man, Harden-Hickey begged: "Let's pretend I'm a king."

But the trouble was, the other boys had grown up and would not pretend.

For some reason his end always reminds me of the closing line of Pinero's play, when the adventuress, Mrs. Tanqueray, kills herself, and her virtuous stepchild says: "If we had only been kinder!"

WINSTON SPENCER CHURCHILL

IN the strict sense of the phrase, a soldier of fortune is a man who for pay, or for the love of adventure, fights under the flag of any country.

In the bigger sense he is the kind of man who in any walk of life makes his own fortune, who, when he sees it coming, leaps to meet it, and turns it to his advantage.

Than Winston Spencer Churchill to-day there are few young men - and he is a very young man - who have met more varying fortunes, and none who has more frequently bent them to his own advancement. To him it has been indifferent whether, at the moment, the fortune seemed good or evil, in the end always it was good.

As a boy officer, when other subalterns were playing polo, and at the Gaiety Theatre attending night school, he ran away to Cuba and fought with the Spaniards. For such a breach of military discipline, any other officer would have been court-martialled. Even his friends feared that by his foolishness his career in the army was at an end. Instead, his escapade was made a question in the House of Commons, and the fact brought him such publicity that the *Daily Graphic* paid him handsomely to write on the Cuban Revolution, and the Spanish Government rewarded him with the Order of Military Merit.

At the very outbreak of the Boer war he was taken prisoner. It seemed a climax of misfortune. With his brother officers he had hoped in that campaign to acquit himself with credit, and that he should lie inactive in Pretoria appeared a terrible calamity. To the others who, through many heart-breaking months, suffered imprisonment, it continued to be a calamity. But within six weeks of his capture Churchill escaped, and, after many adventures, rejoined his own army to find that the calamity had made him a hero.

When after the battle of Omdurman, in his book on "The River War," he attacked Lord Kitchener, those who did not like him, and they were many, said: "That's the end of Winston in the army. He'll never get another chance to criticise K. of K."

But only two years later the chance came, when, no longer a subaltern, but as a member of the House of Commons, he patronized Kitchener by defending him from the attacks of others.

Later, when his assaults upon the leaders of his own party closed to him, even in his own constituency, the Conservative debating clubs, again his ill-wishers said: "This *is* the end. He has ridiculed those who sit in high places. He has offended his cousin and patron, the Duke of Marlborough. Without political friends, without the influence and money of the Marlborough family he is a political nonentity." That was eighteen months ago. To-day, at the age of thirty-two, he is one of the leaders of the Government party, Under-Secretary for the Colonies, and with the Liberals the most popular young man in public life.

Only last Christmas, at a banquet, Sir Edward Grey, the new Foreign Secretary, said of him: "Mr. Winston Churchill has achieved distinction in at least five different careers - as a soldier, a war correspondent, a lecturer, an author, and last, but not least, as a politician. I have understated it even now, for he has achieved two careers as a politician - one on each side of the House. His first career on the Government side was a really distinguished career. I trust the second will be even more distinguished - and more prolonged. The remarkable thing is that he has done all this when, unless appearances very much belie him, he has not reached the age of sixty-four, which is the minimum age at which the politician ceases to be young."

Winston Leonard Spencer Churchill was born thirty-two years ago, in November, 1874. By birth he is half-American. His father was Lord Randolph Churchill, and his mother was Jennie Jerome, of New York. On the father's side he is the grandchild of the seventh Duke of Marlborough, on the distaff side, of Leonard Jerome.

To a student of heredity it would be interesting to try and discover from which of these ancestors Churchill drew those qualities which in him are most prominent, and which have led to his success.

What he owes to his father and mother it is difficult to overestimate, almost as difficult as to overestimate what he has accomplished by his own efforts.

He was not a child born a full-grown genius of commonplace parents. Rather his fate threatened that he should always be known as the son of his father. And certainly it was asking much of a boy that he should live up to a father who was one of the most conspicuous, clever, and erratic statesmen of the later Victorian era, and a mother who is as brilliant as she is beautiful.

For at no time was the American wife content to be merely ornamental. Throughout the political career of her husband she was his helpmate, and as an officer of the Primrose League, as an editor of the *Anglo-Saxon Review*, as, for many hot, weary months in Durban Harbor, the head of the hospital ship *Maine*, she has shown an acute mind and real executive power. At the polls many votes that would not respond to the arguments of the husband, and later of the son, were gained over to the cause by the charm and wit of the American woman.

In his earlier days, if one can have days any earlier than those he now enjoys, Churchill was entirely influenced by two things: the tremendous admiration he felt for his father, which filled him with ambition to follow in his orbit, and the camaraderie of his mother, who treated him less like a mother than a sister and companion.

Indeed, Churchill was always so precocious that I cannot recall the time when he was young enough to be Lady Randolph's son; certainly, I cannot recall the time when she was old enough to be his mother.

When first I knew him he had passed through Harrow and Sandhurst and was a second lieutenant in the Queen's Own Hussars. He was just of age, but appeared much younger.

He was below medium height, a slight, delicate-looking boy; although, as a matter of fact, extremely strong, with blue eyes, many freckles, and hair which threatened to be a decided red, but which now has lost its fierceness. When he spoke it was with a lisp, which also has changed, and which now appears to be merely an intentional hesitation.

His manner of speaking was nervous, eager, explosive. He used many gestures, some of which were strongly reminiscent of his father, of whom he, unlike most English lads, who shy at mentioning a distinguished parent, constantly spoke.

He even copied his father in his little tricks of manner. Standing with hands shoved under the frock-coat and one resting on each hip as though squeezing in the waist line; when seated, resting the elbows on the arms of the chair and nervously locking and unclasping fingers, are tricks common to both.

He then had and still has a most embarrassing habit of asking many questions; embarrassing, sometimes, because the questions are so frank, and sometimes because they lay bare the wide expanse of one's own ignorance.

At that time, although in his twenty-first year, this lad twice had been made a question in the House of Commons.

That in itself had rendered him conspicuous. When you consider out of Great Britain's four hundred million subjects how many live, die, and are buried without at any age having drawn down upon themselves the anger of the House of Commons, to have done so twice, before one has passed his twenty-first year, seems to promise a lurid future.

The first time Churchill disturbed the august assemblage in which so soon he was to become a leader was when he "ragged" a brother subaltern named Bruce and cut up his saddle and accoutrements. The second time was when he ran away to Cuba to fight with the Spaniards.

After this campaign, on the first night of his arrival in London, he made his maiden speech. He delivered it in a place of less dignity than the House of Commons, but one, throughout Great Britain and her colonies, as widely known and as well supported. This was the Empire Music Hall.

At the time Mrs. Ormiston Chant had raised objections to the presence in the Music Hall of certain young women, and had threatened, unless they ceased to frequent its promenade, to have the license of the Music Hall revoked. As a compromise, the management ceased selling liquor, and on the night Churchill visited the place the bar in the promenade was barricaded with scantling and linen sheets. With the thirst of tropical Cuba still upon him, Churchill asked for a drink, which was denied him, and the crusade, which in his absence had been progressing fiercely, was explained. Any one else would have taken no for his answer, and have sought elsewhere for his drink. Not so Churchill. What he did is interesting, because it was so extremely characteristic. Now he would not do it; then he was twenty-one.

He scrambled to the velvet-covered top of the railing which divides the auditorium from the promenade, and made a speech. It was a plea in behalf of his "Sisters, the Ladies of the Empire Promenade."

"Where," he asked of the ladies themselves and of their escorts crowded below him in the promenade, "does the Englishman in London always find a welcome? Where does he first go when, battle-scarred and travel-worn, he reaches home? Who is always there to greet him with a smile, and join him in a drink? Who is ever faithful, ever true - the Ladies of the Empire Promenade."

The laughter and cheers that greeted this, and the tears of the ladies themselves, naturally brought the performance on the stage to a stop, and the vast audience turned in the seats and boxes.

They saw a little red-haired boy in evening clothes, balancing himself on the rail of the balcony, and around him a great crowd, cheering, shouting, and bidding him "Go on!" Churchill turned with delight to the larger audience, and repeated his appeal. The house shook with laughter and applause.

The commissionaires and police tried to reach him and a good-tempered but very determined mob of well-dressed gentlemen and cheering girls fought them back. In triumph Churchill ended his speech by begging his hearers to give "fair play" to the women, and to follow him in a charge upon the barricades.

The charge was instantly made, the barricades were torn down, and the terrified management ordered that drink be served to its victorious patrons.

Shortly after striking this blow for the liberty of others,

Churchill organized a dinner which illustrated the direction in which at that age his mind was working, and showed that his ambition was already abnormal. The dinner was given to those of his friends and acquaintances who "were under twenty-one years of age, and who in twenty years would control the destinies of the British Empire."

As one over the age limit, or because he did not consider me an empire-controlling force, on this great occasion, I was permitted to be present. But except that the number of incipient empire-builders was very great, that they were very happy, and that save the host himself none of them took his idea seriously, I would not call it an evening of historical interest. But the fact is interesting that of all the boys present, as yet, the host seems to be the only one who to any conspicuous extent is disturbing the destinies of Great Britain. However, the others can reply that ten of the twenty years have not yet passed.

When he was twenty-three Churchill obtained leave of absence from his regiment, and as there was no other way open to him to see fighting, as a correspondent he joined the Malakand Field Force in India.

It may be truthfully said that by his presence in that frontier war he made it and himself famous. His book on that campaign is his best piece of war reporting. To the civilian reader it has all the delight of one of Kipling's Indian stories, and to writers on military subjects it is a model. But it is a model very few can follow, and which Churchill himself was unable to follow, for the reason that only once is it given a man to be twenty-three years of age.

The picturesque hand-to-hand fighting, the night attacks, the charges up precipitous hills, the retreats made carrying the wounded under constant fire, which he witnessed and in which he bore his part, he never again can see with the same fresh and enthusiastic eyes. Then it was absolutely new, and the charm of the book and the value of the book are that with the intolerance of youth he attacks in the service evils that older men prefer to let lie, and that with the ingenuousness of youth he tells of things which to the veteran have become unimportant, or which through usage he is no longer even able to see.

In his three later war books, the wonder of it, the horror of it, the quick admiration for brave deeds and daring men, give place, in "The River War," to the critical point of view of the military expert, and in his two books on the Boer war to the rapid impressions of the journalist. In these latter books he tells you of battles he has seen, in the first one he made you see them.

For his services with the Malakand Field Force he received the campaign medal with clasp, and, "in despatches," Brigadier-General Jeffreys praises "the courage and resolution of Lieutenant W. L. S. Churchill, Fourth Hussars, with the force as correspondent of the *Pioneer*."

From the operations around Malakand, he at once joined Sir William Lockhart as orderly officer, and with the Tirah Expedition went through that campaign.

For this his Indian medal gained a second clasp.

This was in the early part of 1898. In spite of the time

taken up as an officer and as a correspondent, he finished his book on the Malakand Expedition and then, as it was evident Kitchener would soon attack Khartum, he jumped across to Egypt and again as a correspondent took part in the advance upon that city.

Thus, in one year, he had seen service in three campaigns.

On the day of the battle his luck followed him. Kitchener had attached him to the Twenty-first Lancers, and it will be remembered the event of the battle was the charge made by that squadron. It was no canter, no easy "pig-sticking"; it was a fight to get in and a fight to get out, with frenzied followers of the Khalifa hanging to the bridle reins, hacking at the horses' hamstrings, and slashing and firing point-blank at the troopers. Churchill was in that charge. He received the medal with clasp.

Then he returned home and wrote "The River War." This book is the last word on the campaigns up the Nile. From the death of Gordon in Khartum to the capture of the city by Kitchener, it tells the story of the many gallant fights, the wearying failures, the many expeditions into the hot, boundless desert, the long, slow progress toward the final winning of the Sudan.

The book made a distinct sensation. It was a work that one would expect from a lieutenant-general, when, after years of service in Egypt, he laid down his sword to pen the story of his life's work. From a Second Lieutenant, who had been on the Nile hardly long enough to gain the desert tan, it was a revelation. As a contribution to military history it was so valuable that for the author it made many admirers, but on account of his criticisms of his superior officers it gained him even more enemies.

This is a specimen of the kind of thing that caused the retired army officer to sit up and choke with apoplexy:

"General Kitchener, who never spares himself, cares little for others. He treated all men like machines, from the private soldiers, whose salutes he disdained, to the superior officers, whom he rigidly controlled. The comrade who had served with him and under him for many years, in peace and peril, was flung aside as soon as he ceased to be of use. The wounded Egyptian and even the wounded British soldier did not excite his interest."

When in the service clubs they read that, the veterans asked each other their favorite question of what is the army coming to, and to their own satisfaction answered it by pointing out that when a lieutenant of twenty-four can reprimand the commanding general the army is going to the dogs.

To the newspapers, hundreds of them, over their own signatures, on the service club stationery, wrote violent, furious letters, and the newspapers themselves, besides the ordinary reviews, gave to the book editorial praise and editorial condemnation.

Equally disgusted were the younger officers of the service. They nicknamed his book "A Subaltern's Advice to Generals," and called Churchill himself a "Medal Snatcher." A medal snatcher is an officer who, whenever there is a rumor of war, leaves his men to the care of any one, and through influence in high places and for the sake of the campaign medal has himself attached to the expeditionary force. But Churchill never was a medal hunter. The routine of barrack life irked him, and in foreign parts he served his country far better than by remaining at home and inspecting awkward squads and attending guard mount. Indeed, the War Office could cover with medals the man who wrote "The Story of the Malakand Field Force" and "The River War" and still be in his debt.

In October, 1898, a month after the battle of Omdurman, Churchill made his debut as a political speaker at minor meetings in Dover and Rotherhithe. History does not record that these first speeches set fire to the Channel. During the winter he finished and published his "River War," and in the August of the following summer, 1899, at a by-election, offered himself as Member of Parliament for Oldham.

In the *Daily Telegraph* his letters from the three campaigns in India and Egypt had made his name known, and there was a general desire to hear him and to see him. In one who had attacked Kitchener of Khartum, the men of Oldham expected to find a stalwart veteran, bearded, and with a voice of command. When they were introduced to a small red-haired boy with a lisp, they refused to take him seriously. In England youth is an unpardonable thing. Lately, Curzon, Churchill, Edward Grey, Hugh Cecil, and others have made it less reprehensible. But, in spite of a vigorous campaign, in which Lady Randolph took an active part, Oldham decided it was not ready to accept young Churchill for a member. Later he was Oldham's only claim to fame.

A week after he was defeated he sailed for South Africa, where war with the Boers was imminent. He had resigned from his regiment and went south as war correspondent for the *Morning Post.*

Later in the war he held a commission as Lieutenant in the South African Light Horse, a regiment of irregular cavalry, and on the staffs of different generals acted as galloper and aide-de-camp. To this combination of duties, which was in direct violation of a rule of the War Office, his brother officers and his fellow correspondents objected; but, as in each of his other campaigns he had played this dual role, the press censors considered it a traditional privilege, and winked at it. As a matter of record, Churchill's soldiering never seemed to interfere with his writing, nor, in a fight, did his duty to his paper ever prevent him from mixing in as a belligerent.

War was declared October 9th, and only a month later, while scouting in the armored train along the railroad line between Pietermaritzburg and Colenso, the cars were derailed and Churchill was taken prisoner.

The train was made up of three flat cars, two armored cars, and between them the engine, with three cars coupled to the cow-catcher and two to the tender.

On the outward trip the Boers did not show themselves, but as soon as the English passed Frere station they rolled a rock on the track at a point where it was hidden by a curve. On the return trip, as the English approached this curve the Boers opened fire with artillery and pompoms. The engineer, in his eagerness to escape, rounded the curve at full speed, and, as the Boers had expected, hit the rock. The three forward cars were derailed, and one of them was thrown across the track, thus preventing the escape of the engine and the two rear cars. From these Captain Haldane, who was in command, with a detachment of the Dublins, kept up a steady fire on the enemy, while Churchill worked to clear the track. To assist him he had a company of Natal volunteers, and those who had not run away of the train hands and break-down crew.

"We were not long left in the comparative safety of a railroad accident," Churchill writes to his paper. "The Boers' guns, swiftly changing their position, reopened fire from a distance of thirteen hundred yards before any one had got out of the stage of exclamations. The tapping rifle-fire spread along the hills, until it encircled the wreckage on three sides, and from some high ground on the opposite side of the line a third field-gun came into action."

For Boer marksmen with Mausers and pompoms, a wrecked railroad train at thirteen hundred yards was as easy a bull's-eye as the hands of the first baseman to the pitcher, and while the engine butted and snorted and the men with their bare bands tore at the massive beams of the freight-car, the bullets and shells beat about them.

"I have had in the last four years many strange and varied experiences," continues young Churchill, "but nothing was so thrilling as this; to wait and struggle among these clanging, rending iron boxes, with the repeated explosions of the shells, the noise of the projectiles striking the cars, the hiss as they passed in the air, the grunting and puffing of the engine - poor, tortured thing, hammered by at least a dozen shells, any one of which, by penetrating the boiler, might have made an end of all - the expectation of destruction as a matter of course, the realization of powerlessness - all this for seventy minutes by the clock, with only four inches of twisted iron between danger, captivity, and shame on one side - and freedom on the other."

The "protected" train had proved a deathtrap, and by the time the line was clear every fourth man was killed or wounded. Only the engine, with the more severely wounded heaped in the cab and clinging to its cowcatcher and foot-rails, made good its escape. Among those left behind, a Tommy, without authority, raised a handkerchief on his rifle, and the Boers instantly ceased firing and came galloping forward to accept surrender. There was a general stampede to escape. Seeing that Lieutenant Franklin was gallantly trying to hold his men, Churchill, who was safe on the engine, jumped from it and ran to his assistance. Of what followed, this is his own account:

"Scarcely had the locomotive left me than I found myself alone in a shallow cutting, and none of our soldiers, who had all surrendered, to be seen. Then suddenly there appeared on the line at the end of the cutting two men not in uniform. 'Plate-layers,' I said to myself, and then, with a surge of realization, 'Boers.' My mind retains a momentary impression of these tall figures, full of animated movement, clad in dark flapping clothes, with slouch, storm-driven hats, posing their rifles hardly a hundred yards away. I turned and ran between the rails of the track, and the only thought I achieved was this: 'Boer marksmanship.'

"Two bullets passed, both within a foot, one on either side. I flung myself against the banks of the cutting. But they gave no cover. Another glance at the figures; one was now kneeling to aim. Again I darted forward. Again two soft kisses sucked in the air, but nothing struck me. I must get out of the cutting - that damnable corridor. I scrambled up the bank. The earth sprang up beside me, and a bullet touched my hand, but outside the cutting was a tiny depression. I crouched in this, struggling to get my wind. On the other side of the railway a horseman galloped up, shouting to me and waving his hand. He was scarcely forty yards off. With a rifle I could have killed him easily. I knew nothing of the white flag, and the bullets had made me savage. I reached down for my Mauser pistol. I had left it in the cab of the engine. Between me and the horseman there was a wire fence. Should I continue to fly? The idea of another shot at such a short range decided me. Death stood before me, grim and sullen; Death without his light-hearted companion, Chance. So I held up my hand, and like Mr. Jorrock's foxes, cried 'Capivy!' Then I was herded with the other prisoners in a miserable group, and about the same time I noticed that my hand was bleeding, and it began to pour with rain.

"Two days before I had written to an officer at home: 'There has been a great deal too much surrendering in this war, and I hope people who do so will not be encouraged.'"

With other officers, Churchill was imprisoned in the State Model Schools, situated in the heart of Pretoria. It was distinctly characteristic that on the very day of his arrival he began to plan to escape.

Toward this end his first step was to lose his campaign hat, which he recognized was too obviously the hat of an English officer. The burgher to whom he gave money to purchase him another innocently brought him a Boer sombrero.

Before his chance to escape came a month elapsed, and the opportunity that then offered was less an opportunity to escape than to get himself shot.

The State Model Schools were surrounded by the children's playgrounds, penned in by a high wall, and at night, while they were used as a prison, brilliantly lighted by electric lights. After many nights of observation, Churchill discovered that while the sentries were pacing their beats there was a moment when to them a certain portion of the wall was in darkness. This was due to cross-shadows cast by the electric lights. On the other side of this wall there was a private house set in a garden filled with bushes. Beyond this was the open street.

To scale the wall was not difficult; the real danger lay in the fact that at no time were the sentries farther away than fifteen yards, and the chance of being shot by one or both of them was excellent. To a brother officer Churchill confided his purpose, and together they agreed that some night when the sentries had turned from the dark spot on the wall they would scale it and drop among the bushes in the garden. After they reached the garden, should they reach it alive, what they were to do they did not know. How they were to proceed through the streets and out of the city, how they were to pass unchallenged under its many electric lights and before the illuminated shop windows, how to dodge patrols, and how to find their way through two hundred and eighty miles of a South African wilderness, through an utterly unfamiliar, unfriendly, and sparsely settled country into Portuguese territory and the coast, they left to chance. But with luck they hoped to cover the distance in a fortnight, begging corn at the Kaffir kraals, sleeping by day, and marching under cover of the darkness.

They agreed to make the attempt on the 11th of December, but on that night the sentries did not move from the only part of the wall that was in shadow. On the night following, at the last moment, something delayed Churchill's companion, and he essayed the adventure alone. He writes: "Tuesday, the 12th! Anything was better than further suspense. Again night came. Again the dinner bell sounded. Choosing my opportunity, I strolled across the quadrangle and secreted myself in one of the offices. Through a chink I watched the sentries. For half an hour they remained stolid and obstructive. Then suddenly one turned and walked up to his comrade and they began to talk. Their backs were turned.

I darted out of my hiding-place and ran to the wall, seized the top with my hands and drew myself up. Twice I let myself down again in sickly hesitation, and then with a third resolve scrambled up. The top was flat. Lying on it, I had one parting glimpse of the sentries, still talking, still with their backs turned, but, I repeat, still fifteen yards away. Then I lowered myself into the adjoining garden and crouched among the shrubs. I was free. The first step had been taken, and it was irrevocable."

Churchill discovered that the house into the garden of which he had so unceremoniously introduced himself was brilliantly lighted, and that the owner was giving a party. At one time two of the guests walked into the garden and stood, smoking and chatting, in the path within a few yards of him.

Thinking his companion might yet join him, for an

hour he crouched in the bushes, until from the other side of the wall he heard the voices of his friend and of another officer.

"It's all up!" his friend whispered. Churchill coughed tentatively. The two voices drew nearer. To confuse the sentries, should they be listening, the one officer talked nonsense, laughed loudly, and quoted Latin phrases, while the other, in a low and distinct voice, said: " I cannot get out. The sentry suspects. It's all up. Can you get back again?"

To go back was impossible. Churchill now felt that in any case he was sure to be recaptured, and decided he would, as he expresses it, at least have a run for his money.

"I shall go on alone," he whispered.

He heard the footsteps of his two friends move away from him across the play yard. At the same moment he stepped boldly out into the garden and, passing the open windows of the house, walked down the gravel path to the street. Not five yards from the gate stood a sentry. Most of those guarding the school-house knew him by sight, but Churchill did not turn his head, and whether the sentry recognized him or not, he could not tell.

For a hundred feet he walked as though on ice, inwardly shrinking as he waited for the sharp challenge, and the rattle of the Mauser thrown to the "Ready." His nerves were leaping, his heart in his throat, his spine of water. And then, as he continued to advance, and still no tumult pursued him, he quickened his pace and turned into one of the main streets of

Pretoria. The sidewalks were crowded with burghers, but no one noticed him. This was due probably to the fact that the Boers wore no distinctive uniform, and that with them in their commandoes were many English Colonials who wore khaki riding breeches, and many Americans, French, Germans, and Russians, in every fashion of semi-uniform.

If observed, Churchill was mistaken for one of these, and the very openness of his movements saved him from suspicion.

Straight through the town he walked until he reached the suburbs, the open veldt, and a railroad track. As he had no map or compass he knew this must be his only guide, but he knew also that two railroads left Pretoria, the one along which he had been captured, to Pietermaritzburg, and the other, the one leading to the coast and freedom. Which of the two this one was he had no idea, but he took his chance, and a hundred yards beyond a station waited for the first outgoing train. About midnight, a freight stopped at the station, and after it had left it and before it had again gathered headway, Churchill swung himself up upon it, and stretched out upon a pile of coal. Throughout the night the train continued steadily toward the east, and so told him that it was the one he wanted, and that he was on his way to the neutral territory of Portugal.

Fearing the daylight, just before the sun rose, as the train was pulling up a steep grade, he leaped off into some bushes. All that day he lay hidden, and the next night he walked. He made but little headway. As all stations and bridges were guarded, he had to make long detours, and the tropical moonlight prevented him from crossing in the open. In this way, sleeping by day, walking by night, begging food from the Kaffirs, five days passed.

Meanwhile, his absence had been at once discovered, and, by the Boers, every effort was being made to retake him. Telegrams giving his description were sent along both railways, three thousand photographs of him were distributed, each car of every train was searched, and in different parts of the Transvaal men who resembled him were being arrested. It was said he had escaped dressed as a woman; in the uniform of a Transvaal policeman whom he had bribed; that he had never left Pretoria, and that in the disguise of a waiter he was concealed in the house of a British sympathizer. On the strength of this rumor the houses of all suspected persons were searched.

In the Volksstem it was pointed out as a significant fact that a week before his escape Churchill had drawn from the library Mill's "Essay on Liberty."

In England and over all British South Africa the escape created as much interest as it did in Pretoria. Because the attempt showed pluck, and because he had outwitted the enemy, Churchill for the time became a sort of popular hero, and to his countrymen his escape gave as much pleasure as it was a cause of chagrin to the Boers.

But as days passed and nothing was heard of him, it was feared he had lost himself in the Machadodorp Mountains, or had succumbed to starvation, or, in the jungle toward the coast, to fever, and congratulations gave way to anxiety.

The anxiety was justified, for at this time Churchill

was in a very bad way. During the month in prison he had obtained but little exercise. The lack of food and of water, the cold by night and the terrific heat by day, the long stumbling marches in the darkness, the mental effect upon an extremely nervous, high-strung organization of being hunted, and of having to hide from his fellow men, had worn him down to a condition almost of collapse.

Even though it were neutral soil, in so exhausted a state he dared not venture into the swamps and waste places of the Portuguese territory; and, sick at heart as well as sick in body, he saw no choice left him save to give himself up.

But before doing so he carefully prepared a tale which, although most improbable, he hoped might still conceal his identity and aid him to escape by train across the border.

One night after days of wandering he found himself on the outskirts of a little village near the boundary line of the Transvaal and Portuguese territory. Utterly unable to proceed further, he crawled to the nearest zinc-roofed shack, and, fully prepared to surrender, knocked at the door. It was opened by a rough-looking, bearded giant, the first white man to whom in many days Churchill had dared address himself.

To him, without hope, he feebly stammered forth the speech he had rehearsed. The man listened with every outward mark of disbelief. At Churchill himself he stared with open suspicion. Suddenly he seized the boy by the shoulder, drew him inside the hut, and barred the door.

"You needn't lie to me," he said. "You are Winston Churchill, and I - am the only Englishman in this village."

The rest of the adventure was comparatively easy. The next night his friend in need, an engineer named Howard, smuggled Churchill Into a freight-car, and hid him under sacks of some soft merchandise.

At Komatie-Poort, the station on the border, for eighteen hours the car in which Churchill lay concealed was left in the sun on a siding, and before it again started it was searched, but the man who was conducting the search lifted only the top layer of sacks, and a few minutes later Churchill heard the hollow roar of the car as it passed over the bridge, and knew that he was across the border.

Even then he took no chances, and for two days more lay hidden at the bottom of the car.

When at last he arrived in Lorenzo Marques he at once sought out the English Consul, who, after first mistaking him for a stoker from one of the ships in the harbor, gave him a drink, a bath, and a dinner.

As good luck would have it, the *Induna* was leaving that night for Durban, and, escorted by a body-guard of English residents armed with revolvers, and who were taking no chances of his recapture by the Boer agents, he was placed safely on board. Two days later he arrived at Durban, where he was received by the Mayor, the populace, and a brass band playing: "Britons Never, Never, Never shall be Slaves!"

For the next month Churchill was bombarded by letters

and telegrams from every part of the globe, some invited him to command filibustering expeditions, others sent him woollen comforters, some forwarded photographs of himself to be signed, others photographs of themselves, possibly to be admired, others sent poems, and some bottles of whiskey.

One admirer wrote: "My congratulations on your wonderful and glorious deeds, which will send such a thrill of pride and enthusiasm through Great Britain and the United States of America, that the Anglo-Saxon race will be irresistible."

Lest so large an order as making the Anglo-Saxon race irresistible might turn the head of a subaltern, an antiseptic cablegram was also sent him, from London, reading:

"Best friends here hope you won't go making further ass of yourself.

"McNEILL."

One day in camp we counted up the price per word of this cablegram, and Churchill was delighted to find that it must have cost the man who sent it five pounds.

On the day of his arrival in Durban, with the cheers still in the air, Churchill took the first train to "the front," then at Colenso. Another man might have lingered. After a month's imprisonment and the hardships of the escape, he might have been excused for delaying twenty-four hours to taste the sweets of popularity and the flesh-pots of the Queen Hotel. But if the reader has followed this brief biography he will know that to have done so would have been out of the part. This characteristic of Churchill's to get on to the next thing explains his success. He has no time to waste on postmortems, he takes none to rest on his laurels.

As a war correspondent and officer he continued with Buller until the relief of Ladysmith, and with Roberts until the fall of Pretoria. He was in many actions, in all the big engagements, and came out of the war with another medal and clasps for six battles.

On his return to London he spent the summer finishing his second book on the war, and in October at the general election as a "khaki" candidate, as those were called who favored the war, again stood for Oldham. This time, with his war record to help him, he wrested from the Liberals one of Oldham's two seats. He had been defeated by thirteen hundred votes; he was elected by a majority of two hundred and twenty-seven.

The few months that intervened between his election and the opening of the new Parliament were snatched by Churchill for a lecturing tour at home, and in the United States and Canada. His subject was the war and his escape from Pretoria.

When he came to this country half of the people here were in sympathy with the Boers, and did not care to listen to what they supposed would be a strictly British version of the war. His manager, without asking permission of those whose names he advertised, organized for Churchill's first appearance in various cities, different reception committees.

Some of those whose names, without their consent,

were used for these committees, wrote indignantly to the papers, saying that while for Churchill, personally, they held every respect, they objected to being used to advertise an anti-Boer demonstration.

While this was no fault of Churchill's, who, until he reached this country knew nothing of it, it was neither for him nor for the success of his tour the best kind of advance work.

During the fighting to relieve Ladysmith, with General Buller's force, Churchill and I had again been together, and later when I joined the Boer army, at the Zand River Battle, the army with which he was a correspondent had chased the army with which I was a correspondent, forty miles. I had been one of those who refused to act on his reception committee, and he had come to this country with a commission from twenty brother officers to shoot me on sight. But in his lecture he was using the photographs I had taken of the scene of his escape, and which I had sent him from Pretoria as a souvenir, and when he arrived I was at the hotel to welcome him, and that same evening three hours after midnight he came, in a blizzard, pounding at our door for food and drink. What is a little thing like a war between friends?

During his "tour," except of hotels, parlor-cars, and "Lyceums," he saw very little of this country or of its people, and they saw very little of him. On the trip, which lasted about two months, he cleared ten thousand dollars. This, to a young man almost entirely dependent for an income upon his newspaper work and the sale of his books, nearly repaid him for the two months of "one night stands." On his return to London he took his seat in the new Parliament.

It was a coincidence that he entered Parliament at the same age as did his father. With two other members, one born six days earlier than himself, he enjoyed the distinction of being among the three youngest members of the new House.

The fact did not seem to appall him. In the House it is a tradition that young and ambitious members sit "below" the gangway; the more modest and less assured are content to place themselves "above" it, at a point farthest removed from the leaders.

On the day he was sworn in there was much curiosity to see where Churchill would elect to sit. In his own mind there was apparently no doubt. After he had taken the oath, signed his name, and shaken the hand of the Speaker, without hesitation he seated himself on the bench next to the Ministry. Ten minutes later, so a newspaper of the day describes it, he had cocked his hat over his eyes, shoved his hands into his trousers pockets, and was lolling back eying the veterans of the House with critical disapproval.

His maiden speech was delivered in May, 1901, in reply to David Lloyd George, who had attacked the conduct of British soldiers in South Africa. Churchill defended them, and in a manner that from all sides gained him honest admiration. In the course of the debate he produced and read a strangely apropos letter which, fifteen years before, had been written by his father to Lord Salisbury. His adroit use of this filled H. W. Massingham, the editor of the *Daily News*, with enthusiasm. Nothing in parliamentary tactics, he declared, since Mr. Gladstone died, had been so clever. He proclaimed that Churchill would be Premier. John Dillon, the Nationalist leader, said he never before had seen a young man, by means of his maiden effort, spring into the front rank of parliamentary speakers. He promised that the Irish members would ungrudgingly testify to his ability and honesty of purpose. Among others to at once recognize the rising star was T. P. O'Connor, himself for many years of the parliamentary firmament one of the brightest stars. In *M. A. P.* he wrote: "I am inclined to think that the dash of American blood which he has from his mother has been an improvement on the original stock, and that Mr. Winston Churchill may turn out to be a stronger and abler politician than his father."

It was all a part of Churchill's "luck" that when he entered Parliament the subject in debate was the conduct of the war.

Even in those first days of his career in the House, in debates where angels feared to tread, he did not hesitate to rush in, but this subject was one on which he spoke with knowledge. Over the older men who were forced to quote from hearsay or from what they had read, Churchill had the tremendous advantage of being able to protest: "You only read of that. I was there. I saw it."

In the House he became at once one of the conspicuous and picturesque figures, one dear to the heart of the caricaturist, and one from the strangers' gallery most frequently pointed out. He was called "the spoiled child of the House," and there were several distinguished gentlemen who regretted they were forced to spare the rod. Broderick, the Secretary for War, was one of these. Of him and of his recruits in South Africa, Churchill spoke with the awful frankness of the *enfant terrible*. And although he addressed them more with sorrow than with anger, to Balfour and Chamberlain he daily administered advice and reproof, while mere generals and field-marshals, like Kitchener and Roberts, blushing under new titles, were held up for public reproof and briefly but severely chastened. Nor, when he saw Lord Salisbury going astray, did he hesitate in his duty to the country, but took the Prime Minister by the hand and gently instructed him in the way he should go. This did not tend to make him popular, but in spite of his unpopularity, in his speeches against national extravagancies he made so good a fight that he forced the Government, unwillingly, to appoint a committee to investigate the need of economy. For a beginner this was a distinct triumph.

With Lord Hugh Cecil, Lord Percy, Ian Malcolm, and other clever young men, he formed inside the Conservative Party a little group that in its obstructive and independent methods was not unlike the Fourth Party of his father. From its leader and its filibustering, guerilla-like tactics the men who composed it were nicknamed the "Hughligans." The Hughligans were the most active critics of the Ministry and of all in their own party, and as members of the Free Food League they bitterly attacked the fiscal proposals of Mr. Chamberlain. When Balfour made Chamberlain's fight for fair trade, or for what virtually was protection, a measure of the Conservatives, the lines of party began to break, and men were no longer Conservatives or Liberals, but Protectionists or Free Traders.

Against this Churchill daily protested, against Chamberlain, against his plan, against that plan being adopted by the Tory Party. By tradition, by inheritance, by instinct, Churchill was a Tory.

"I am a Tory," he said, "and I have as much right in the party as has anybody else, certainly as much as certain people from Birmingham. They can't turn us out, and we, the Tory Free Traders, have as much right to dictate the policy of the Conservative Party as have any reactionary Fair Traders." In 1904 the Conservative Party already recognized Churchill as one working outside the breastworks. Just before the Easter vacation of that year, when he rose to speak a remarkable demonstration was made against him by his Unionist colleagues, all of them rising and leaving the House.

To the Liberals who remained to hear him he stated that if to his constituents his opinions were obnoxious, he was ready to resign his seat. It then was evident he would go over to the Liberal Party. Some thought he foresaw which way the tidal wave was coming, and to being slapped down on the beach and buried in the sand, he preferred to be swept forward on its crest. Others believed he left the Conservatives because he could not honestly stomach the taxed food offered by Mr. Chamberlain.

In any event, if he were to be blamed for changing from one party to the other, he was only following the distinguished example set him by Gladstone, Disraeli, Harcourt, and his own father.

It was at the time of this change that he was called "the best hated man in England," but the Liberals welcomed him gladly, and the National Liberal Club paid him the rare compliment of giving in his honor a banquet. There were present two hundred members. Up to that time this dinner was the most marked testimony to his importance in the political world. It was about then, a year since, that he prophesied: "Within nine months there will come such a tide and deluge as will sweep through England and Scotland, and completely wash out and effect a much-needed spring cleaning in Downing Street."

When the deluge came, at Manchester, Mr. Balfour was defeated, and Churchill was victorious, and when the new Government was formed the tidal wave landed Churchill in the office of Under-Secretary for the Colonies.

While this is being written the English papers say that within a month he again will be promoted. For this young man of thirty the only promotion remaining is a position in the Cabinet, in which august body men of fifty are considered young.

His is a picturesque career. Of any man of his few years speaking our language, his career is probably the most picturesque. And that he is half an American gives all of us an excuse to pretend we share in his successes.

CAPTAIN PHILO NORTON McGIFFIN

IN the Chinese-Japanese War the battle of the Yalu was the first battle fought between warships of modern make, and, except on paper, neither the men who made them nor the men who fought them knew what the ships could do, or what they might not do. For years every naval power had been building these new engines of war, and in the battle which was to test them the whole world was interested. But in this battle Americans had a special interest, a human, family interest, for the reason that one of the Chinese squadron, which was matched against some of the same vessels of Japan which lately swept those of Russia from the sea, was commanded by a young graduate of the American Naval Academy. This young man, who, at the time of the battle of the Yalu, was thirty-three years old, was Captain Philo Norton McGiffin. So it appears that five years before our fleet sailed to victory in Manila Bay another graduate of Annapolis, and one twenty years younger than in 1898 was Admiral Dewey, had commanded in action a modern battleship, which, in tonnage, in armament, and in the number of the ships' company, far outclassed Dewey's *Olympia*.

McGiffin, who was born on December 13, 1860, came of fighting stock. Back in Scotland the family is descended from the Clan MacGregor and the Clan MacAlpine.

"These are Clan-Alpine's warriors true,
And, Saxon - I am Roderick Dhu."

McGiffin's great-grandfather, born in Scotland, emigrated to this country and settled in "Little Washington," near Pittsburg, Pa. In the Revolutionary War he was a soldier. Other relatives fought in the War of 1812, one of them holding a commission as major. McGiffin's own father was Colonel Norton McGiffin, who served in the Mexican War, and in the Civil War was Lieutenant-Colonel of the Eighty-fifth Pennsylvania Volunteers. So McGiffin inherited his love for arms.

In Washington he went to the high school and at the Washington Jefferson College had passed through his freshman year. But the honors that might accrue to him if he continued to live on in the quiet and pretty old town of Washington did not tempt him. To escape into the world he wrote his Congressman, begging him to obtain for him an appointment to Annapolis. The Congressman liked the letter, and wrote Colonel McGiffin to ask if the application of his son had his approval. Colonel McGiffin was willing, and in 1877 his son received his commission as cadet midshipman. I knew McGiffin only as a boy with whom in vacation time I went coon hunting in the woods outside of Washington. For his age he was a very tall boy, and in his midshipman undress uniform, to my youthful eyes, appeared a most bold and adventurous spirit.

At Annapolis his record seems to show he was pretty much like other boys. According to his classmates, with all of whom I find he was very popular, he stood high in the practical studies, such as seamanship, gunnery, navigation, and steam engineering, but in all else he was near the foot of the class, and in whatever escapade was risky and reckless he was always one of the leaders. To him discipline was extremely irksome. He could maintain it among others, but when it applied to himself it bored him. On the floor of the Academy building on which was his room there was a pyramid of cannon balls - relics of the War of 1812. They stood at the head of the stairs, and one warm night, when he could not sleep, he decided that no one else should do so, and, one by one, rolled the cannon balls down the stairs. They tore away the banisters and bumped through the wooden steps and leaped off into the lower halls. For any one who might think of ascending to discover the motive power back of the bombardment they were extremely dangerous. But an officer approached McGiffin in the rear, and, having been caught in the act, he was sent to the prison ship. There he made good friends with his jailer, an old man-of-warsman named "Mike." He will be remembered by many naval officers who as midshipmen served on the *Santee*. McGiffin so won over Mike that when he left the ship he carried with him six charges of gunpowder. These he loaded into the six big guns captured in the Mexican War, which lay on the grass in the centre of the Academy grounds, and at midnight on the eve of July 1st he fired a salute. It aroused the entire garrison, and for a week the empty window frames kept the glaziers busy.

About 1878 or 1879 there was a famine in Ireland. The people of New York City contributed provisions for the sufferers, and to carry the supplies to Ireland the Government authorized the use of the old

Constellation. At the time the voyage was to begin each cadet was instructed to consider himself as having been placed in command of the *Constellation* and to write a report on the preparations made for the voyage, on the loading of the vessel, and on the distribution of the stores. This exercise was intended for the instruction of the cadets; first in the matter of seamanship and navigation, and second in making official reports. At that time it was a very difficult operation to get a gun out of the port of a vessel where the gun was on a covered deck. To do this the necessary tackles had to be rigged from the yard-arm and the yard and mast properly braced and stayed, and then the lower block of the tackle carried in through the gun port, which, of course, gave the fall a very bad reeve. The first part of McGiffin's report dealt with a new method of dismounting the guns and carrying them through the gun ports, and so admirable was his plan, so simple and ingenious, that it was used whenever it became necessary to dismount a gun from one of the old sailing ships. Having, however, offered this piece of good work, McGiffin's report proceeded to tell of the division of the ship into compartments that were filled with a miscellaneous assortment of stores, which included the old "fifteen puzzles," at that particular time very popular. The report terminated with a description of the joy of the famished Irish as they received the puzzle-boxes. At another time the cadets were required to write a report telling of the suppression of the insurrection on the Isthmus of Panama. McGiffin won great praise for the military arrangements and disposition of his men, but, in the same report, he went on to describe how he armed them with a new gun known as Baines's Rhetoric and told of the havoc he wrought in the enemy's ranks when he fired these guns loaded with similes and metaphors and hyperboles.

Of course, after each exhibition of this sort he was sent to the *Santee* and given an opportunity to meditate.

On another occasion, when one of the instructors lectured to the cadets, he required them to submit a written statement embodying all that they could recall of what had been said at the lecture. One of the rules concerning this report provided that there should be no erasures or interlineations, but that when mistakes were made the objectionable or incorrect expressions should be included within parentheses; and that the matter so enclosed within parentheses would not be considered a part of the report. McGiffin wrote an excellent *resume* of the lecture, but he interspersed through it in parentheses such words as "applause," "cheers," "cat-calls," and "groans," and as these words were enclosed within parentheses he insisted that they did not count, and made a very fair plea that he ought not to be punished for words which slipped in by mistake, and which he had officially obliterated by what he called oblivion marks.

He was not always on mischief bent. On one occasion, when the house of a professor caught fire, McGiffin ran into the flames and carried out two children, for which act he was commended by the Secretary of the Navy.

It was an act of Congress that determined that the career of McGiffin should be that of a soldier of fortune. This was a most unjust act, which provided that only as many midshipmen should receive commissions as on the warships there were actual vacancies. In those days, in 1884, our navy was very small. To-day there is hardly a ship having her full complement of officers, and the difficulty is not to get rid of those we have educated, but to get officers to educate. To the many boys who, on the promise that they would be officers of the navy, had worked for four years at the Academy and served two years at sea, the act was most unfair. Out of a class of about ninety, only the first twelve were given commissions and the remaining eighty turned adrift upon the uncertain seas of civil life. As a sop, each was given one thousand dollars.

McGiffin was not one of the chosen twelve. In the final examinations on the list he was well toward the tail. But without having studied many things, and without remembering the greater part of them, no one graduates from Annapolis, even last on the list; and with his one thousand dollars in cash, McGiffin had also this six years of education at what was then the best naval college in the world. This was his only asset - his education - and as in his own country it was impossible to dispose of it, for possible purchasers he looked abroad.

At that time the Tong King war was on between France and China, and he decided, before it grew rusty, to offer his knowledge to the followers of the Yellow Dragon. In those days that was a hazard of new fortunes that meant much more than it does now. To-day the East is as near as San Francisco; the Japanese-Russian War, our occupation of the Philippines, the part played by our troops in the Boxer trouble, have made the affairs of China part of the daily reading of every one. Now, one can step into a brass bed at Forty-second Street and in four days at the Coast get into another brass bed, and in twelve more be spinning down the Bund of Yokohama in a rickshaw. People go to Japan for the winter months as they used to go to Cairo.

But in 1885 it was no such light undertaking, certainly not for a young man who had been brought up in the quiet atmosphere of an inland town, where generations of his family and other families had lived and intermarried, content with their surroundings.

With very few of his thousand dollars left him, McGiffin arrived in February, 1885, in San Francisco. From there his letters to his family give one the picture of a healthy, warm-hearted youth, chiefly anxious lest his mother and sister should "worry." In our country nearly every family knows that domestic tragedy when the son and heir "breaks home ties," and starts out to earn a living; and if all the world loves a lover, it at least sympathizes with the boy who is "looking for a job." The boy who is looking for the job may not think so, but each of those who has passed through the same hard place gives him, if nothing else, his good wishes. McGiffin's letters at this period gain for him from those who have had the privilege to read them the warmest good feeling.

They are filled with the same cheery optimism, the same slurring over of his troubles, the same homely jokes, the same assurances that he is feeling "bully," and that it all will come out right, that every boy, when he starts out in the world, sends back to his mother.

"I am in first-rate health and spirits, so I don't want you to fuss about me. I am big enough and ugly enough to scratch along somehow, and I will not starve."

To his mother he proudly sends his name written in Chinese characters, as he had been taught to write it by the Chinese Consul-General in San Francisco, and a pen-picture of two elephants. "I am going to bring you home *two* of these," he writes, not knowing that in the strange and wonderful country to which he is going elephants are as infrequent as they are in Pittsburg.

He reached China in April, and from Nagasaki on his way to Shanghai the steamer that carried him was chased by two French gunboats. But, apparently much to his disappointment, she soon ran out of range of their guns. Though he did not know it then, with the enemy he had travelled so far to fight this was his first and last hostile meeting; for already peace was in the air.

Of that and of how, in spite of peace, he obtained the "job" he wanted, he must tell you himself in a letter home:

TIEN-TSIN, CHINA, April 13, 1885.

"MY DEAR MOTHER - I have not felt much in the humor for writing, for I did not know what was going to happen. I spent a good deal of money coming out, and when I got here, I knew, unless something turned up, I was a gone coon. We got off Taku forts Sunday evening and the next morning we went inside; the channel is very narrow and sown with torpedoes. We struck one - an electric one - in coming up, but it didn't go off. We were until 10.30 P.M. in coming up to Tien-Tsin - thirty miles in a straight line, but nearly seventy by the river, which is only about one hundred feet wide - and we grounded ten times.

"Well - at last we moored and went ashore. Brace Girdle, an engineer, and I went to the hotel, and the first thing we heard was - that *peace was declared!* I went back on board ship, and I didn't sleep much - I never was so blue in my life. I knew if they didn't want me that I might as well give up the ghost, for I could never get away from China. Well - I worried around all night without sleep, and in the morning I felt as if I had been drawn through a knot-hole. I must have lost ten pounds. I went around about 10 A.M. and gave my letters to Pethick, an American U. S. Vice-Consul and interpreter to Li Hung Chang. He said he would fix them for me. Then I went back to the ship, and as our captain was going up to see Li Hung Chang, I went along out of desperation. We got in, and after a while were taken in through corridor after corridor of the Viceroy's palace until we got into the great Li, when we sat down and had tea and tobacco and talked through an interpreter. When it came my turn he asked: 'Why did you come to China?' I said: 'To enter the Chinese service for the war.' 'How do you expect to enter?' 'I expect *you* to give me a commission!' 'I have no place to offer you.' 'I think you have - I have come all the way from America to get it.' 'What would you like?' 'I would like to get the new torpedo-boat and go down the Yang-tse-Kiang to the blockading squadron.' 'Will you do that?' 'Of course.'

"He thought a little and said: 'I will see what can be done. Will you take $100 a month for a start?' I said: 'That depends.' (Of course I would take it.) Well, after parley, he said he would put me on the flagship, and if I did well he would promote me. Then he looked at me and said: 'How old are you ?' When I told him I was twenty-four I thought he would faint - for in China a man is a *boy* until he is over thirty. He said I would *never* do - I was a child. I could not know anything at all. I could not convince him, but at last he compromised - I was to pass an examination at the Arsenal at the Naval College, in all branches, and if they passed me I would have a show. So we parted. I reported for examination next day, but was put off - same the next day. But to-day I was told to come, and sat down to a stock of foolscap, and had a pretty stiff exam. I am only just through. I had seamanship, gunnery, navigation, nautical astronomy, algebra, geometry, trigonometry, conic sections, curve tracing, differential and integral calculus. I had only three questions out of five to answer in each branch, but in the first three I answered all five. After that I only had time for three, but at the end he said I need not finish, he was perfectly satisfied. I had done remarkably well, and he would report to the Viceroy to-morrow. He examined my first papers - seamanship - said I was *perfect* in it, so I will get *along*, you need not fear. I told the Consul - he was very well pleased - he is a nice man.

"I feel pretty well now - have had dinner and am smoking a good Manila cheroot. I wrote hard all day, wrote fifteen sheets of foolscap and made about a dozen drawings - got pretty tired.

"I have had a hard scramble for the service and only got in by the skin of my teeth. I guess I will go to bed - I will sleep well to-night - Thursday.

"I did not hear from the Naval Secretary, Tuesday, so yesterday morning I went up to the Admiralty and sent in my card. He came out and received me very well - said I had passed a 'very splendid examination'; had been recommended very strongly to the Viceroy, who was very much pleased; that the Director of the Naval College over at the Arsenal had wanted me and would I go over at once? I *would*. It was about five miles. We (a friend, who is a great rider here) went on steeplechase ponies - we were ferried across the Pei Ho in a small scow and then had a long ride. There *is* a path - but Pritchard insisted on taking all the ditches, and as my pony jumped like a cat, it wasn't nice at first, but I didn't squeal and kept my seat and got the swing of it at last and rather liked it. I think I will keep a horse here - you can hire one and a servant together for $7 a month; that is $5.60 of our money, and pony and man found in everything.

"Well - at last we got to the Arsenal - a place about four miles around, fortified, where all sorts of arms - cartridges, shot and shell, engines, and *everything* - are made. The Naval College is inside surrounded by a moat and wall. I thought to myself, if the cadet here is like to the thing I used to be at the U. S. N. A. *that* won't keep him in. I went through a lot of yards till I was ushered into a room finished in black ebony and was greeted very warmly by the Director. We took seats on a raised platform - Chinese style and pretty soon an interpreter came, one of the Chinese professors, who was educated abroad, and we talked and drank tea. He said I had done well, that he had the authority of the Viceroy to take me there as 'Professor' of seamanship and gunnery; in addition I might be required to teach navigation or nautical astronomy, or drill the cadets in infantry, artillery, and fencing. For this I was to receive what would be in our money $1,800 per annum, as near as we can compare it, paid in gold each month. Besides, I will have a house furnished for my use, and it is their intention, as soon as I *show* that I *know* something, to considerably increase my pay. They asked the Viceroy to give me 130 T per month (about $186) and house, but the Viceroy said I was *but a boy*; that I had seen no years and had only come here a week ago with no one to vouch for me, and that I might turn out an impostor. But he would risk 100 T on me anyhow, and as soon as I was reported favorably on by the college I would be raised - the agreement is to be for three years. For a few months I am to command a training ship - an ironclad that is in dry dock at present, until a captain in the English Navy comes out, who has been sent for to command her.

"*So Here I am* - twenty-four years old and captain of a man-of-war - a better one than any in our own navy - only for a short time, of course, but I would be a pretty long time before I would command one at home. Well - I accepted and will enter on my duties in a week, as soon as my house is put in order. I saw it - it has a long veranda, very broad; with flower garden, apricot trees, etc., just covered with blossoms; a wide hall on the front, a room about 18x15, with a 13-foot ceiling; then back another rather larger, with a cupola skylight in the centre, where I am going to put a shelf with flowers. The Government is to furnish the house with bed, tables, chairs, sideboards, lounges, stove for kitchen. I have grates (American) in the room, but I don't need them. We have snow, and a good deal of ice in winter, but the thermometer never gets below zero. I have to supply my own crockery. I will have two servants and cook; I will only get one and the cook first - they only cost $4 to $5.50 per month, and their board amounts to very little. I can get along, don't you think so? Now I want you to get Jim to pack up all my professional works on gunnery, surveying, seamanship, mathematics, astronomy, algebra, geometry, trigonometry, conic sections, calculus, mechanics, and *every* book of that description I own, including those paperbound 'Naval Institute' papers, and put them in a box, together with any photos, etc., you think I would like - I have none of you or Pa or the family (including Carrie) - and send to me.

"I just got in in time - didn't I? Another week would have been too late. My funds were getting low; I would not have had *anything* before long. The U. S. Consul, General Bromley, is much pleased. The interpreter says it was all in the way I did with the Viceroy in the interview.

"I will have a chance to go to Peking and later to a tiger hunt in Mongolia, but for the present I am going to study, work, and *stroke* these mandarins till I get a raise. I am the only instructor in both seamanship and gunnery, and I must know *everything*, both practically and theoretically. But it will be good for me and the only thing is, that if I were put back into the Navy I would be in a dilemma. I think I will get my 'influence' to work, and I want you people at home to look out, and in case I *am* - if it were represented to the Sec. that my position here was giving me an immense lot of practical knowledge professionally - more than I could get on a ship at sea - I think he would give me two years' leave on half or quarter pay. Or, I would be willing to do without pay - only to be kept on the register in my rank.

"I will write more about this. Love to all."

It is characteristic of McGiffin that in the very same letter in which he announces he has entered foreign service he plans to return to that of his own country.

This hope never left him. You find the same homesickness for the quarterdeck of an American man-of-war all through his later letters. At one time a bill to reinstate the midshipmen who had been cheated of their commissions was introduced into Congress. Of this McGiffin writes frequently as "our bill." "It may pass," he writes, "but I am tired hoping. I have hoped so long. And if it should," he adds anxiously, "there may be a time limit set in which a man must rejoin, or lose his chance, so do not fail to let me know as quickly as you can." But the bill did not pass, and McGiffin never returned to the navy that had cut him adrift. He settled down at Tien-Tsin and taught the young cadets how to shoot. Almost all of those who in the Chinese-Japanese War served as officers were his pupils. As the navy grew, he grew with it, and his position increased in importance. More Mexican dollars per month, more servants, larger houses, and buttons of various honorable colors were given him, and, in return, he established for China a modem naval college patterned after our own. In those days throughout China and Japan you could find many of these foreign advisers. Now, in Japan, the Hon. W. H. Dennison of the Foreign Office, one of our own people, is the only foreigner with whom the Japanese have not parted, and in China there are none. Of all of those who have gone none served his employers more faithfully than did McGiffin. At a time when every official robbed the people and the Government, and when "squeeze" or "graft" was recognized as a perquisite, McGiffin's hands were clean. The shells purchased for the Government by him were not loaded with black sand, nor were the rifles fitted with barrels of iron pipe. Once a year he celebrated the Thanksgiving Day of his own country by inviting to a great dinner all the Chinese naval officers who had been at least in part educated in America. It was a great occasion, and to enjoy it officers used to come from as far as Port Arthur, Shanghai, and Hong-Kong. So fully did some of them appreciate the efforts of their host that previous to his annual dinner, for twenty-four hours, they delicately starved themselves.

During ten years McGiffin served as naval constructor and professor of gunnery and seamanship, and on board ships at sea gave practical demonstrations in the handling of the new cruisers. In 1894 he applied for leave, which was granted, but before he had sailed for home war with Japan was declared and he withdrew his application. He was placed as second in command on board the *Chen Yuen*, a seven-thousand-ton battleship, a sister ship to the *Ting Yuen*, the flagship of Admiral Ting Ju Chang. On the memorable 17th of September, 1894, the battle of the Yalu was fought, and so badly were the Chinese vessels hammered that the Chinese navy, for the time being, was wiped out of existence.

From the start the advantage was with the Japanese fleet. In heavy guns the Chinese were the better armed, but in quick-firing guns the Japanese were vastly superior, and while the Chinese battleships *Ting Yuen* and *Chen Yuen*, each of 7,430 tons, were superior to any of the Japanese warships, the three largest of which were each of 4,277 tons, the gross tonnage of the Japanese fleet was 36,000 to 21,000 of the Chinese. During the progress of the battle the ships engaged on each side numbered an even dozen, but at the very start, before a decisive shot was fired by either contestant, the *Tsi Yuen*, 2,355 tons, and *Kwan Chiae*, 1,300 tons, ran away, and before they had time to get into the game the *Chao Yung* and *Yang Wei* were in flames and had fled to the nearest land. So the battle was fought by eight Chinese ships against twelve of the Japanese. Of the Chinese vessels, the flagship, commanded by Admiral Ting, and her sister ship, which immediately after the beginning of the fight was for four hours commanded by McGiffin, were the two chief aggressors, and in consequence received the fire of the entire Japanese squadron. Toward the end of the fight, which without interruption lasted for five long hours, the Japanese did not even consider the four smaller ships of the enemy, but, sailing around the two ironclads in a circle, fired only at them. The Japanese themselves testified that these two ships never lost their formation, and that when her sister ironclad was closely pressed the *Chen Yuen*, by her movements and gun practice, protected the *Ting Yuen*, and, in fact, while she could not prevent the heavy loss the fleet encountered, preserved it from annihilation. During the fight this ship was almost continuously on fire, and was struck by every kind of projectile, from the thirteen-inch Canet shells to a rifle bullet, four hundred times. McGiffin himself was so badly wounded, so beaten about by concussions, so burned, and so bruised by steel splinters, that his health and eyesight were forever wrecked. But he brought the *Chen Yuen* safely into Port Arthur and the remnants of the fleet with her.

On account of his lack of health he resigned from the Chinese service and returned to America. For two years he lived in New York City, suffering in body without cessation the most exquisite torture. During that time his letters to his family show only tremendous courage. On the splintered, gaping deck of the *Chen Yuen*, with the fires below it, and the shells bursting upon it, he had shown to his Chinese crew the courage of the white man who knew he was responsible for them and for the honor of their country. But far greater and more difficult was the courage he showed while alone in the dark sick-room, and in the private wards of the hospitals.

In the letters he dictates from there he still is concerned only lest those at home shall "worry"; he reassures them with falsehoods, jokes at their fears; of the people he can see from the window of the hospital tells them foolish stories; for a little boy who has been kind he asks them to send him his Chinese postage stamps; he plans a trip he will take with them when he is stronger, knowing he never will be stronger. The doctors had urged upon him a certain operation, and of it to a friend he wrote: "I know that I will have to have a piece about three inches square cut out of my skull, and this nerve cut off near the middle of the brain, as well as my eye taken out (for a couple of hours only, provided it is not mislaid, and can be found). Doctor - and his crowd show a bad memory for failures. As a result of this operation others have told me - I forget the percentage of deaths, which does not matter, but - that a large percentage have become insane. And some lost their sight."

While threatened with insanity and complete blindness, and hourly from his wounds suffering a pain drugs could not master, he dictated for the *Century Magazine* the only complete account of the battle of the Yalu. In a letter to Mr. Richard Watson Gilder he writes: "...my eyes are troubling me. I cannot see even what I am writing now, and am getting the article under difficulties. I yet hope to place it in your hands by the 21st, still, if my eyes grow worse - "

"Still, if my eyes grow worse - "

The unfinished sentence was grimly prophetic.

Unknown to his attendants at the hospital, among the papers in his despatch-box he had secreted his service revolver. On the morning of the 11th of February, 1897, he asked for this box, and on some pretext sent the nurse from the room. When the report of the pistol brought them running to his bedside, they found the pain-driven body at peace, and the tired eyes dark forever.

In the article in the *Century* on the battle of the Yalu, he had said:

"Chief among those who have died for their country is Admiral Ting Ju Chang, a gallant soldier and true gentleman. Betrayed by his countrymen, fighting against odds, almost his last official act was to stipulate for the lives of his officers and men. His own he scorned to save, well knowing that his ungrateful country would prove less merciful than his honorable foe. Bitter, indeed, must have been the reflections of the old, wounded hero, in that midnight hour, as he drank the poisoned cup that was to give him rest."

And bitter indeed must have been the reflections of the young wounded American, robbed, by the parsimony of his country, of the right he had earned to serve it, and who was driven out to give his best years and his life for a strange people under a strange flag.

GENERAL WILLIAM WALKER, THE KING OF THE FILIBUSTERS

IT is safe to say that to members of the younger generation the name of William Walker conveys absolutely nothing. To them, as a name, "William Walker" awakens no pride of race or country. It certainly does not suggest poetry and adventure. To obtain a place in even this group of Soldiers of Fortune, William Walker, the most distinguished of all American Soldiers of Fortune, the one who but for his own countrymen would have single-handed attained the most far-reaching results, had to wait his turn behind adventurers of other lands and boy officers of his own. And yet had this man with the plain name, the name that to-day means nothing, accomplished what he adventured, he would on this continent have solved the problem of slavery, have established an empire in Mexico and in Central America, and, incidentally, have brought us into war with all of Europe. That is all he would have accomplished.

In the days of gold in San Francisco among the "Forty-niners" William Walker was one of the most famous, most picturesque and popular figures. Jack Oakhurst, gambler; Colonel Starbottle, duellist; Yuba Bill, stage-coach driver, were his contemporaries. Bret Harte was one of his keenest admirers, and in two of his stories, thinly disguised under a more appealing name, Walker is the hero. When, later, Walker came to New York City, in his honor Broadway from the Battery to Madison Square was bedecked with flags and arches. "It was roses, roses all the way." The house-tops rocked and swayed.

In New Orleans, where in a box at the opera he made his first appearance, for ten minutes the performance came to a pause, while the audience stood to salute him.

This happened less than fifty years ago, and there are men who as boys were out with "Walker of Nicaragua," and who are still active in the public life of San Francisco and New York.

Walker was born in 1824, in Nashville, Tenn. He was the oldest son of a Scotch banker, a man of a deeply religious mind, and interested in a business which certainly is removed, as far as possible, from the profession of arms. Indeed, few men better than William Walker illustrate the fact that great generals are born, not trained. Everything in Walker's birth, family tradition, and education pointed to his becoming a member of one of the "learned" professions. It was the wish of his father that he should be a minister of the Presbyterian Church, and as a child he was trained with that end in view. He himself preferred to study medicine, and after graduating at the University of Tennessee, at Edinburgh he followed a course of lectures, and for two years travelled in Europe, visiting many of the great hospitals.

Then having thoroughly equipped himself to practise as a physician, after a brief return to his native city, and as short a stay in Philadelphia, he took down his shingle forever, and proceeded to New Orleans to study law. In two years he was admitted to the bar of Louisiana. But because clients were few, or because the red tape of the law chafed his spirit, within a year, as already he had abandoned the Church and Medicine, he abandoned his law practice and became an editorial writer on the New Orleans *Crescent*. A year later the restlessness which had rebelled against the grave professions led him to the gold fields of California, and San Francisco. There, in 1852, at the age of only twenty-eight, as editor of the San Francisco *Herald*, Walker began his real life which so soon was to end in both disaster and glory.

Up to his twenty-eighth year, except in his restlessness, nothing in his life foreshadowed what was to follow. Nothing pointed to him as a man for whom thousands of other men, from every capital of the world, would give up their lives.

Negatively, by abandoning three separate callings, and in making it plain that a professional career did not appeal to him, Walker had thrown a certain sidelight on his character; but actively he never had given any hint that under the thoughtful brow of the young doctor and lawyer there was a mind evolving schemes of empire, and an ambition limited only by the two great oceans.

Walker's first adventure was undoubtedly inspired by and in imitation of one which at the time of his arrival in San Francisco had just been brought to a disastrous end. This was the De Boulbon expedition into Mexico. The Count Gaston Raoulx de Raousset-Boulbon was a young French nobleman and Soldier of Fortune, a *chasseur d'Afrique*, a duellist, journalist, dreamer, who came to California to dig gold. Baron Harden-Hickey, who was born in San Francisco a few years after Boulbon at the age of thirty was shot in Mexico, also was inspired to dreams of conquest by this same gentleman adventurer.

Boulbon was a young man of large ideas. In the rapid growth of California he saw a threat to Mexico and proposed to that government, as a "buffer" state between the two republics, to form a French colony in the Mexican State of Sonora. Sonora is that part of Mexico which directly joins on the south with our State of Arizona. The President of Mexico gave Boulbon permission to attempt this, and in 1852 he landed at Guaymas in the Gulf of California with two hundred and sixty well-armed Frenchmen. The ostensible excuse of Boulbon for thus invading foreign soil was his contract with the President under which his "emigrants" were hired to protect other foreigners working in the "Restauradora" mines from the attacks of Apache Indians from our own Arizona. But there is evidence that back of Boulbon was the French Government, and that he was attempting, in his small way, what later was attempted by Maximilian, backed by a French army corps and Louis Napoleon, to establish in Mexico an empire under French protection. For both the filibuster and the emperor the end was the same; to be shot by the fusillade against a church wall.

In 1852, two years before Boulbon's death, which was the finale to his second filibustering expedition into Sonora, he wrote to a friend in Paris: "Europeans are disturbed by the growth of the United States. And rightly so. Unless she be dismembered; unless a powerful rival be built up beside her ($i.e.$, France in Mexico), America will become, through her commerce, her trade, her population, her geographical position upon two oceans, the inevitable mistress of the world. In ten years Europe dare not fire a shot without her permission. As I write fifty Americans prepare to sail for Mexico and go perhaps to victory. *Voila les Etats-Unis.*"

These fifty Americans who, in the eyes of Boulbon, threatened the peace of Europe, were led by the ex-doctor, ex-lawyer, ex-editor, William Walker, *aged twenty-eight years.* Walker had attempted but had failed to obtain from the Mexican Government such a contract as the one it had granted De Boulbon. He accordingly sailed without it, announcing that, whether the Mexican Government asked him to do so or not, he would see that the women and children on the border of Mexico and Arizona were protected from massacre by the Indians. It will be remembered that when Dr. Jameson raided the Transvaal he also went to protect "women and children" from massacre by the Boers. Walker's explanation of his expedition, in his own words, is as follows. He writes in the third person: "What Walker saw and heard satisfied him that a comparatively small body of Americans might gain a position on the Sonora frontier and protect the families on the border from the Indians, and such an act would be one of humanity whether or not sanctioned by the Mexican Government. The condition of the upper part of Sonora was at that time, and still is [he was writing eight years later, in 1860], a disgrace to the civilization of the continent...and the people of the United States were more immediately responsible before the world for the Apache outrages. Northern Sonora was in fact, more under the dominion of the Apaches than under the laws of Mexico, and the contributions of the Indians were collected with greater regularity and certainty than the dues of the tax-gatherers. The state of this region furnished the best defence for any American aiming to settle there without the formal consent of Mexico; and, although political changes would certainly have followed the establishment of a colony, they might be justified by the plea that any social organization, no matter how secured, is preferable to that in which individuals and families are altogether at the mercy of savages."

While at the time of Jameson's raid the women and children in danger of massacre from the Boers were as many as there are snakes in Ireland, at the time of Walker's raid the women and children were in danger from the Indians, who as enemies, as Walker soon discovered, were as cruel and as greatly to be feared as he had described them.

But it was not to save women and children that Walker sought to conquer the State of Sonora. At the time of his expedition the great question of slavery was acute; and if in the States next to be admitted to the Union slavery was to be prohibited, the time had come, so it seemed to this statesman of twenty-eight years, when the South must extend her boundaries, and for her slaves find an outlet in fresh territory. Sonora already joined Arizona. By conquest her territory could easily be extended to meet Texas. As a matter of fact, strategically the spot selected by William Walker for the purpose for which he desired it was almost perfect. Throughout his brief career one must remember that the spring of all his acts was this dream of an empire where slavery would be recognized. His mother was a slave-holder. In Tennessee he had been born and bred surrounded by slaves. His youth and manhood had been spent in Nashville and New Orleans. He believed as honestly, as fanatically in the right to hold slaves as did his father in the faith of the Covenanters. To-day one reads his arguments in favor of slavery with the most curious interest. His appeal to the humanity of his reader, to his heart, to his sense of justice, to his fear of God, and to his belief in the Holy Bible not to abolish slavery, but to continue it, to this generation is as amusing as the topsy-turvyisms of Gilbert or Shaw. But to the young man himself slavery was a sacred institution, intended for the betterment of mankind, a God-given benefit to the black man and a God-given right of his white master.

White brothers in the South, with perhaps less exalted motives, contributed funds to fit out Walker's expedition, and in October, 1852, with forty-five men, he landed at Cape St. Lucas, at the extreme point of Lower California. Lower California, it must be remembered, in spite of its name, is not a part of our California, but then was, and still is, a part of Mexico. The fact that he was at last upon the soil of the enemy caused Walker to throw off all pretence; and instead of hastening to protect women and children, he sailed a few miles farther up the coast to La Paz. With his forty-five followers he raided the town, made the Governor a prisoner, and established a republic with himself as President. In a proclamation he declared the people free of the tyranny of Mexico. They had no desire to be free, but Walker was determined, and, whether they liked it or not, they woke up to find themselves an independent republic. A few weeks later, although he had not yet set foot there, Walker annexed on paper the State of Sonora, and to both States gave the name of the Republic of Sonora.

As soon as word of this reached San Francisco, his

friends busied themselves in his behalf, and the danger-loving and adventurous of all lands were enlisted as "emigrants" and shipped to him in the bark *Anita*.

Two months later, in November, 1852, three hundred of these joined Walker. They were as desperate a band of scoundrels as ever robbed a sluice, stoned a Chinaman, or shot a "Greaser." When they found that to command them there was only a boy, they plotted to blow up the magazine in which the powder was stored, rob the camp, and march north, supporting themselves by looting the ranches. Walker learned of their plot, tried the ringleaders by court-martial, and shot them. With a force as absolutely undisciplined as was his, the act required the most complete personal courage. That was a quality the men with him could fully appreciate. They saw they had as a leader one who could fight, and one who would punish. The majority did not want a leader who would punish so when Walker called upon those who would follow him to Sonora to show their hands, only the original forty-five and about forty of the later recruits remained with him. With less than one hundred men he started to march up the Peninsula through Lower California, and so around the Gulf to Sonora.

From the very start the filibusters were overwhelmed with disaster. The Mexicans, with Indian allies, skulked on the flanks and rear. Men who in the almost daily encounters were killed fell into the hands of the Indians, and their bodies were mutilated. Stragglers and deserters were run to earth and tortured. Those of the filibusters who were wounded died from lack of medical care. The only instruments they possessed with which to extract the arrow-heads were probes made from ramrods filed to a point. Their only food was the cattle they killed on the march. The army was barefoot, the Cabinet in rags, the President of Sonora wore one boot and one shoe.

Unable to proceed farther, Walker fell back upon San Vincente, where he had left the arms and ammunition of the deserters and a rear-guard of eighteen men. He found not one of these to welcome him. A dozen had deserted, and the Mexicans had surprised the rest, lassoing them and torturing them until they died. Walker now had but thirty-five men. To wait for further re-enforcements from San Francisco, even were he sure that re-enforcements would come, was impossible. He determined by forced marches to fight his way to the boundary line of California. Between him and safety were the Mexican soldiers holding the passes, and the Indians hiding on his flanks. When within three miles of the boundary line, at San Diego, Colonel Melendrez, who commanded the Mexican forces, sent in a flag of truce, and offered, if they would surrender, a safe-conduct to all of the survivors of the expedition except the chief. But the men who for one year had fought and starved for Walker, would not, within three miles of home, abandon him.

Melendrez then begged the commander of the United States troops to order Walker to surrender. Major McKinstry, who was in command of the United States Army Post at San Diego, refused. For him to cross the line would be a violation of neutral territory. On Mexican soil he would neither embarrass the ex-President of Sonora nor aid him; but he saw to it that if the filibusters reached American soil, no Mexican or Indian should follow them.

Accordingly, on the imaginary boundary he drew up his troop, and like an impartial umpire awaited the result. Hidden behind rocks and cactus, across the hot, glaring plain, the filibusters could see the American flag, and the gay, fluttering guidons of the cavalry. The sight gave them heart for one last desperate spurt. Melendrez also appreciated that for the final attack the moment had come. As he charged, Walker, apparently routed, fled, but concealed in the rocks behind him he had stationed a rear-guard of a dozen men. As Melendrez rode into this ambush the dozen riflemen emptied as many saddles, and the Mexicans and Indians stampeded. A half hour later, footsore and famished, the little band that had set forth to found an empire of slaves, staggered across the line and surrendered to the forces of the United States.

Of this expedition James Jeffrey Roche says, in his "Byways of War," which is of all books published about Walker the most intensely and fascinatingly interesting and complete: "Years afterward the peon herdsman or prowling Cocupa Indian in the mountain by-paths stumbled over the bleaching skeleton of some nameless one whose resting-place was marked by no cross or cairn, but the Colts revolver resting beside his bones spoke his country and his occupation - the only relic of the would-be conquistadores of the nineteenth century."

Under parole to report to General Wood, commanding the Department of the Pacific, the filibusters were sent by sailing vessel to San Francisco, where their leader was tried for violating the neutrality laws of the United States, and acquitted.

Walker's first expedition had ended in failure, but for

him it had been an opportunity of tremendous experience, as active service is the best of all military academies, and for the kind of warfare he was to wage, the best preparation. Nor was it inglorious, for his fellow survivors, contrary to the usual practice, instead of in bar-rooms placing the blame for failure upon their leader, stood ready to fight one and all who doubted his ability or his courage. Later, after five years, many of these same men, though ten to twenty years his senior, followed him to death, and never questioned his judgment nor his right to command.

At this time in Nicaragua there was the usual revolution. On the south the sister republic of Costa Rica was taking sides, on the north Honduras was landing arms and men. There was no law, no government. A dozen political parties, a dozen commanding generals, and not one strong man.

In the editorial rooms of the San Francisco *Herald*, Walker, searching the map for new worlds to conquer, rested his finger upon Nicaragua.

In its confusion of authority he saw an opportunity to make himself a power, and in its tropical wealth and beauty, in the laziness and incompetence of its inhabitants, he beheld a greater, fairer, more kind Sonora. On the Pacific side from San Francisco he could re-enforce his army with men and arms; on the Caribbean side from New Orleans he could, when the moment arrived, people his empire with slaves.

The two parties at war in Nicaragua were the Legitimists and the Democrats. Why they were at war it is not necessary to know. Probably Walker did not know; it is not likely that they themselves knew. But from the leader of the Democrats Walker obtained a contract to bring to Nicaragua three hundred Americans, who were each to receive several hundred acres of land, and who were described as "colonists liable to military duty." This contract Walker submitted to the Attorney-General of the State and to General Wood, who once before had acquitted him of filibustering; and neither of these Federal officers saw anything which seemed to give them the right to interfere. But the rest of San Francisco was less credulous, and the "colonists" who joined Walker had a very distinct idea that they were not going to Nicaragua to plant coffee or to pick bananas.

In May, 1855, just a year after Walker and his thirty-three followers had surrendered to the United States troops at San Diego, with fifty new recruits and seven veterans of the former expedition he sailed from San Francisco in the brig *Vesta*, and in five weeks, after a weary and stormy voyage, landed at Realejo. There he was met by representatives of the Provisional Director of the Democrats, who received the Californians warmly.

Walker was commissioned a colonel, Achilles Kewen, who had been fighting under Lopez in Cuba, a lieutenant-colonel, and Timothy Crocker, who had served under Walker in the Sonora expedition, a major. The corps was organized as an independent command and was named "La Falange Americana." At this time the enemy held the route to the Caribbean, and Walker's first orders were to dislodge him.

Accordingly, a week after landing with his fifty-seven Americans and one hundred and fifty native troops, Walker sailed in the *Vesta* for Brito, from which port he marched upon Rivas, a city of eleven thousand people and garrisoned by some twelve hundred of the enemy.

The first fight ended in a complete and disastrous fiasco. The native troops ran away, and the Americans surrounded by six hundred of the Legitimists' soldiers, after defending themselves for three hours behind some adobe huts, charged the enemy and escaped into the jungle. Their loss was heavy, and among the killed were the two men upon whom Walker chiefly depended: Kewen and Crocker. The Legitimists placed the bodies of the dead and wounded who were still living on a pile of logs and burned them. After a painful night march, Walker, the next day, reached San Juan on the coast, and, finding a Costa Rican schooner in port, seized it for his use. At this moment, although Walker's men were defeated, bleeding, and in open flight, two "gringos " picked up on the beach of San Juan, "the Texan Harry McLeod and the Irishman Peter Burns," asked to be permitted to join him.

"It was encouraging," Walker writes, "for the soldiers to find that some besides themselves did not regard their fortunes as altogether desperate, and small as was this addition to their number it gave increased moral as well as material strength to the command."

Sometimes in reading history it would appear as though for success the first requisite must be an utter lack of humor, and inability to look upon what one is attempting except with absolute seriousness. With forty men Walker was planning to conquer and rule Nicaragua, a country with a population of two hundred and fifty thousand souls and as large as the combined area of Massachusetts, Vermont, Rhode Island, New

Hampshire, and Connecticut. And yet, even seven years later, he records without a smile that two beach-combers gave his army "moral and material strength." And it is most characteristic of the man that at the moment he was rejoicing over this addition to his forces, to maintain discipline two Americans who had set fire to the houses of the enemy he ordered to be shot. A weaker man would have repudiated the two Americans, who, in fact, were not members of the Phalanx, and trusted that their crimes would not be charged against him. But the success of Walker lay greatly in his stern discipline. He tried the men, and they confessed to their guilt. One got away; and, as it might appear that Walker had connived at his escape, to the second man was shown no mercy. When one reads how severe was Walker in his punishments, and how frequently the death penalty was invoked by him against his own few followers, the wonder grows that these men, as independent and as unaccustomed to restraint as were those who first joined him, submitted to his leadership. One can explain it only by the personal quality of Walker himself.

Among these reckless, fearless outlaws, who, despising their allies, believed and proved that with his rifle one American could account for a dozen Nicaraguans, Walker was the one man who did not boast or drink or gamble, who did not even swear, who never looked at a woman, and who, in money matters, was scrupulously honest and unself-seeking. In a fight, his followers knew that for them he would risk being shot just as unconcernedly as to maintain his authority he would shoot one of them.

Treachery, cowardice, looting, any indignity to women, he punished with death; but to the wounded, either of his own or of the enemy's forces, he was as gentle as a nursing sister and the brave and able he rewarded with instant promotion and higher pay. In no one trait was he a demagogue. One can find no effort on his part to ingratiate himself with his men. Among the officers of his staff there were no favorites. He messed alone, and at all times kept to himself. He spoke little, and then with utter lack of self-consciousness. In the face of injustice, perjury, or physical danger, he was always calm, firm, dispassionate. But it is said that on those infrequent occasions when his anger asserted itself, the steady steel-gray eyes flashed so menacingly that those who faced them would as soon look down the barrel of his Colt.

The impression one gets of him gathered from his recorded acts, from his own writings, from the writings of those who fought with him, is of a silent, student-like young man believing religiously in his "star of destiny"; but, in all matters that did not concern himself, possessed of a grim sense of fun. The sayings of his men that in his history of the war he records, show a distinct appreciation of the Bret Harte school of humor. As, for instance, when he tells how he wished to make one of them a drummer boy and the Californian drawled: "No, thanks, colonel; I never seen a picture of a battle yet that the first thing in it wasn't a dead drummer boy with a busted drum."

In Walker the personal vanity which is so characteristic of the soldier of fortune was utterly lacking. In a land where a captain bedecks himself like a field-marshal, Walker wore his trousers stuffed in his boots, a civilian's blue frock-coat, and the slouch hat of the period, with, for his only ornament, the red ribbon of the Democrats. The authority he wielded did not depend upon braid or buttons, and only when going into battle did he wear his sword. In appearance he was slightly built, rather below the medium height, smooth shaven, and with deep-set gray eyes. These eyes apparently, as they gave him his nickname, were his most marked feature.

His followers called him, and later, when he was thirty-two years old, he was known all over the United States as the "Gray-Eyed Man of Destiny."

From the first Walker recognized that in order to establish himself in Nicaragua he must keep in touch with all possible recruits arriving from San Francisco and New York, and that to do this he must hold the line of transit from the Caribbean Sea to the Pacific. At this time the sea routes to the gold-fields were three: by sailing vessel around the Cape, one over the Isthmus of Panama, and one, which was the shortest, across Nicaragua. By a charter from the Government of Nicaragua, the right to transport passengers across this isthmus was controlled by the Accessory Transit Company, of which the first Cornelius Vanderbilt was president. His company owned a line of ocean steamers both on the Pacific side and on the Atlantic side. Passengers *en route* from New York to the gold-fields were landed by these latter steamers at Greytown on the west coast of Nicaragua, and sent by boats of light draught up the San Juan River to Lake Nicaragua. There they were met by larger lake steamers and conveyed across the lake to Virgin Bay. From that point, in carriages and on mule back, they were carried twelve miles overland to the port of San Juan del Sud on the Pacific Coast, where they boarded the company's steamers to San Francisco.

During the year of Walker's occupation the number of passengers crossing Nicaragua was an average of about two thousand a month.

It was to control this route that immediately after his first defeat Walker returned to San Juan del Sud, and in a smart skirmish defeated the enemy and secured possession of Virgin Bay, the halting place for the passengers going east or west. In this fight Walker was outnumbered five to one, but his losses were only three natives killed and a few Americans wounded. The Legitimists lost sixty killed and a hundred wounded. This proportion of losses shows how fatally effective was the rifle and revolver fire of the Californians. Indeed, so wonderful was it that when some years ago I visited the towns and cities captured by the filibusters, I found that the marksmanship of Walker's Phalanx was still a tradition. Indeed, thanks to the filibusters, to-day in any part of Central America a man from the States, if in trouble, has only to show his gun. No native will wait for him to fire it.

After the fight at Virgin Bay, Walker received from California fifty recruits - a very welcome addition to his force, and as he now commanded about one hundred and twenty Americans, three hundred Nicaraguans, under a friendly native, General Valle, and two brass cannon, he decided to again attack Rivas. Rivas is on the lake just above Virgin Bay; still further up is Granada, which was the head-quarters of the Legitimists.

Fearing Walker's attack upon Rivas, the Legitimist troops were hurried south from Granada to that city, leaving Granada but slightly protected.

Through intercepted letters Walker learned of this and determined to strike at Granada. By night, in one of the lake steamers, he skirted the shore, and just before daybreak, with fires banked and all lights out, drew up to a point near the city. The day previous the Legitimists had gained a victory, and, as good luck or Walker's "destiny" would have it, the night before Granada had been celebrating the event. Much joyous dancing and much drinking of aguardiente had buried the inhabitants in a drugged slumber. The garrison slept, the sentries slept, the city slept. But when the convent bells called for early mass, the air was shaken with sharp reports that to the ears of the Legitimists were unfamiliar and disquieting. They were not the loud explosions of their own muskets nor of the smooth bores of the Democrats. The sounds were sharp and cruel like the crack of a whip. The sentries flying from their posts disclosed the terrifying truth. "The Filibusteros!" they cried. Following them at a gallop came Walker and Valle and behind them the men of the awful Phalanx, whom already the natives had learned to fear: the bearded giants in red flannel shirts who at Rivas on foot had charged the artillery with revolvers, who at Virgin Bay when wounded had drawn from their boots glittering bowie knives and hurled them like arrows, who at all times shot with the accuracy of the hawk falling upon a squawking hen.

There was a brief terrified stand in the Plaza, and then a complete rout. As was their custom, the native Democrats began at once to loot the city. But Walker put his sword into the first one of these he met, and ordered the Americans to arrest all others found stealing, and to return the goods already stolen. Over a hundred political prisoners in the cartel were released by Walker, and the ball and chain to which each was fastened stricken off. More than two-thirds of them at once enlisted under Walker's banner.

He now was in a position to dictate to the enemy his own terms of peace, but a fatal blunder on the part of Parker H. French, a lieutenant of Walker's, postponed peace for several weeks, and led to unfortunate reprisals. French had made an unauthorized and unsuccessful assault on San Carlos at the eastern end of the lake, and the Legitimists retaliated at Virgin Bay by killing half a dozen peaceful passengers, and at San Carlos by firing at a transit steamer. For this the excuse of the Legitimists was, that now that Walker was using the lake steamers as transports it was impossible for them to know whether the boats were occupied by his men or neutral passengers. As he could not reach the guilty ones, Walker held responsible for their acts their secretary of state, who at the taking of Granada was among the prisoners. He was tried by court-martial and shot, "a victim of the new interpretation of the principles of constitutional government." While this act of Walker's was certainly stretching the theory of responsibility to the breaking point, its immediate effect was to bring about a hasty surrender and a meeting between the generals of the two political parties. Thus, four months after Walker and his fifty-seven followers landed in Nicaragua, a suspension of hostilities was arranged, and the side for which the Americans had fought was in power. Walker was made commander-in-chief of an army of twelve hundred men with salary of six thousand dollars a year. A man named Rivas was appointed temporary president.

To Walker this pause in the fight was most welcome. It gave him an opportunity to enlist recruits and to organize his men for the better accomplishment of what was the real object of his going to Nicaragua. He now had under him a remarkable force, one of the most effective known to military history. For although six months had not yet passed, the organization he now commanded was as unlike the Phalanx of the fifty-eight adventurers who were driven back at Rivas, as were Falstaff's followers from the regiment of picked men commanded by Colonel Roosevelt. Instead of the undisciplined and lawless now being in the majority, the ranks were filled with the pick of the California mining camps, with veterans of the Mexican War, with young Southerners of birth and spirit, and with soldiers of fortune from all of the great armies of Europe.

In the Civil War, which so soon followed, and later in the service of the Khedive of Egypt, were several of Walker's officers, and for years after his death there was no war in which one of the men trained by him in the jungles of Nicaragua did not distinguish himself. In his memoirs, the Englishman, General Charles Frederic Henningsen, writes that though he had taken part in some of the greatest battles of the Civil War he would pit a thousand men of Walker's command against any five thousand Confederate or Union soldiers. And General Henningsen was one who spoke with authority. Before he joined Walker he had served in Spain under Don Carlos, in Hungary under Kossuth, and in Bulgaria.

Of Walker's men, a regiment of which he commanded, he writes: "I often have seen them march with a broken or compound fractured arm in splints, and using the other to fire the rifle or revolver. Those with a fractured thigh or wounds which rendered them incapable of removal, shot themselves. Such men do not turn up in the average of everyday life, nor do I ever expect to see their like again. All military science failed on a suddenly given field before such assailants, who came at a run to close with their revolvers and who thought little of charging a gun battery, pistol in hand."

Another graduate of Walker's army was Captain Fred Townsend Ward, a native of Salem, Mass., who after the death of Walker organized and led the ever victorious army that put down the Tai-Ping rebellion, and performed the many feats of martial glory for which Chinese Gordon received the credit. In Shanghai, to the memory of the filibuster, there are to-day two temples in his honor.

Joaquin Miller, the poet, miner, and soldier, who but recently was a picturesque figure on the hotel porch at Saratoga Springs, was one of the young Californians who was "out with Walker," and who later in his career by his verse helped to preserve the name of his beloved commander. I. C. Jamison, living to-day in Guthrie, Oklahoma, was a captain under Walker. When war again came, as it did within four months, these were the men who made Walker President of Nicaragua.

During the four months in all but title he had been president, and as such he was recognized and feared. It was against him, not Rivas, that in February, 1856, the neighboring republic of Costa Rica declared war. For three months this war continued with varying fortunes until the Costa Ricans were driven across the border.

In June of the same year Rivas called a general election for president, announcing himself as the candidate of the Democrats. Two other Democrats also presented themselves, Salazar and Ferrer. The

Legitimists, recognizing in their former enemy the real ruler of the country, nominated Walker. By an overwhelming majority he was elected, receiving 15,835 votes to 867 cast for Rivas. Salazar received 2,087; Ferrer, 4,447.

Walker now was the legal as well as the actual ruler of the country, and at no time in its history, as during Walker's administration, was Nicaragua governed so justly, so wisely, and so well. But in his success the neighboring republics saw a menace to their own independence. To the four other republics of Central America the five-pointed blood-red star on the flag of the filibusters bore a sinister motto: "Five or None." The meaning was only too unpleasantly obvious. At once, Costa Rica on the south, and Guatemala, Salvador, and Honduras from the north, with the malcontents of Nicaragua, declared war against the foreign invader. Again Walker was in the field with opposed to him 21,000 of the allies. The strength of his own force varied. On his election as president the backbone of his army was a magnificently trained body of veterans to the number of 2,000. This was later increased to 3,500, but it is doubtful if at any one time it ever exceeded that number. His muster and hospital rolls show that during his entire occupation of Nicaragua there were enlisted, at one time or another, under his banner 10,000 men. While in his service, of this number, by hostile shots or fever, 5,000 died.

To describe the battles with the allies would be interminable and wearying. In every particular they are much alike: the long silent night march, the rush at daybreak, the fight to gain strategic positions either of the barracks, or of the Cathedral in the Plaza, the hand-to-hand fighting from behind barricades and adobe walls. The out-come of these fights sometimes varied, but the final result was never in doubt, and had no outside influences intervened, in time each republic in Central America would have come under the five-pointed star.

In Costa Rica there is a marble statue showing that republic represented as a young woman with her foot upon the neck of Walker. Some night a truth-loving American will place a can of dynamite at the foot of that statue, and walk hurriedly away. Unaided, neither Costa Rica nor any other Central American republic could have driven Walker from her soil. His downfall came through his own people, and through an act of his which provoked them.

When Walker was elected president he found that the Accessory Transit Company had not lived up to the terms of its concession with the Nicaraguan Government. His efforts to hold it to the terms of its concession led to his overthrow. By its charter the Transit Company agreed to pay to Nicaragua ten thousand dollars annually and ten per cent. of the net profits; but the company, whose history the United States Minister, Squire, characterized as "an infamous career of deception and fraud," manipulated its books in such a fashion as to show that there never were any profits. Doubting this, Walker sent a commission to New York to investigate. The commission discovered the fraud and demanded in back payments two hundred and fifty thousand dollars. When the company refused to pay this, as security for the debt Walker seized its steamers, wharves, and storehouses, revoked its charter, and gave a new charter to two of its directors, Morgan and Garrison, who, in San Francisco, were working against Vanderbilt. In doing this, while he was legally in the right, he committed a fatal error. He had made a powerful enemy of Vanderbilt, and he had shut off his only lines of communication with the United States. For, enraged at the presumption of the filibuster president, Vanderbilt withdrew his ocean steamers, thus leaving Walker without men or ammunition, and as isolated as though upon a deserted island. He possessed Vanderbilt's boats upon the San Juan River and Nicaragua Lake, but they were of use to him only locally.

His position was that of a man holding the centre span of a bridge of which every span on either side of him has been destroyed.

Vanderbilt did not rest at withdrawing his steamers, but by supporting the Costa Ricans with money and men, carried the war into Central America. From Washington he fought Walker through Secretary of State Marcy, who proved a willing tool.

Spencer and Webster, and the other soldiers of fortune employed by Vanderbilt, closed the route on the Caribbean side, and the man-of-war *St. Marys*, commanded by Captain Davis, was ordered to San Juan on the Pacific side. The instructions given to Captain Davis were to aid the allies in forcing Walker out of Nicaragua. Walker claims that these orders were given to Marcy by Vanderbilt and by Marcy to Commodore Mervin, who was Marcy's personal friend and who issued them to Davis. Davis claims that he acted only in the interest of humanity to save Walker in spite of himself. In any event, the result was the same. Walker, his force cut down by hostile shot and fever and desertion, took refuge in Rivas, where he was besieged by the allied armies. There was no bread in the city. The men were living on horse and mule meat. There was no salt. The hospital was filled with wounded and those stricken with fever.

Captain Davis, in the name of humanity, demanded Walker's surrender to the United States. Walker told him he would not surrender, but that if the time came when he found he must fly, he would do so in his own little schooner of war, the *Granada*, which constituted his entire navy, and in her, as a free man, take his forces where he pleased. Then Davis informed Walker that the force Walker had sent to recapture the Greytown route had been defeated by the janizaries of Vanderbilt; that the steamers from San Francisco, on which Walker now counted to bring him reenforcements, had also been taken off the line, and finally that it was his "unalterable and deliberate intention" to seize the *Granada*. On this point his orders left him no choice. The *Granada* was the last means of transportation still left to Walker. He had hoped to make a sortie and on board her to escape from the country. But with his ship taken from him and no longer able to sustain the siege of the allies, he surrendered to the forces of the United States. In the agreement drawn up by him and Davis, Walker provided for the care, by Davis, of the sick and wounded, for the protection after his departure of the natives who had fought with him, and for the transportation of himself and officers to the United States.

On his arrival in New York he received a welcome such as later was extended to Kossuth, and, in our own day, to Admiral Dewey. The city was decorated with flags and arches; and banquets, fetes, and public meetings were everywhere held in his honor. Walker received these demonstrations modestly, and on every public occasion announced his determination to return to the country of which he was the president, and from which by force he had been driven. At Washington, where he went to present his claims, he received scant encouragement. His protest against Captain Davis was referred to Congress, where it was allowed to die.

Within a month Walker organized an expedition with which to regain his rights in Nicaragua, and as, in his new constitution for that country, he had annulled the old law abolishing slavery, among the slave-holders of the South he found enough money and recruits to enable him to at once leave the United States. With one hundred and fifty men he sailed from New Orleans and landed at San del Norte on the Caribbean side. While he formed a camp on the harbor of San Juan, one of his officers, with fifty men, proceeded up the river and, capturing the town of Castillo Viejo and four of the Transit steamers, was in a fair way to obtain possession of the entire route. At this moment upon the scene arrived the United States frigate *Wabash* and Hiram Paulding, who landed a force of three hundred and fifty blue-jackets with howitzers, and turned the guns of his frigate upon the camp of the President of Nicaragua. Captain Engel, who presented the terms of surrender to Walker, said to him: "General, I am sorry to see you here. A man like you is worthy to command better men." To which Walker replied grimly: "If I had a third the number you have brought against me, I would show you which of us two commands the better men."

For the third time in his history Walker surrendered to the armed forces of his own country.

On his arrival in the United States, in fulfilment of his parole to Paulding, Walker at once presented himself at Washington a prisoner of war. But President Buchanan, although Paulding had acted exactly as Davis had done, refused to support him, and in a message to Congress declared that that officer had committed a grave error and established an unsafe precedent.

On the strength of this Walker demanded of the United States Government indemnity for his losses, and that it should furnish him and his followers transportation even to the very camp from which its representatives had torn him. This demand, as Walker foresaw, was not considered seriously, and with a force of about one hundred men, among whom were many of his veterans, he again set sail from New Orleans. Owing to the fact that, to prevent his return, there now were on each side of the Isthmus both American and British men-of-war, Walker, with the idea of reaching Nicaragua by land, stopped off at Honduras. In his war with the allies the Honduranians had been as savage in their attacks upon his men as even the Costa Ricans, and finding his old enemies now engaged in a local revolution, on landing, Walker declared for the weaker side and captured the important seaport of Trujillo. He no sooner had taken it than the British warship *Icarus* anchored in the harbor, and her commanding officer, Captain Salmon, notified Walker that the British Government held a mortgage on the revenues of the port, and that to protect the interests of his Government he intended to take the town. Walker answered that he had made Trujillo a free port, and that Great Britain's claims no longer existed.

The British officer replied that if Walker surrendered

himself and his men he would carry them as prisoners to the United States, and that if he did not, he would bombard the town. At this moment General Alvarez, with seven hundred Honduranians, from the land side surrounded Trujillo, and prepared to attack. Against such odds by sea and land Walker was helpless, and he determined to fly. That night, with seventy men, he left the town and proceeded down the coast toward Nicaragua. The *Icarus*, having taken on board Alvarez, started in pursuit. The President of Nicaragua was found in a little Indian fishing village, and Salmon sent in his shore-boats and demanded his surrender. On leaving Trujillo, Walker had been forced to abandon all his ammunition save thirty rounds a man, and all of his food supplies excepting two barrels of bread. On the coast of this continent there is no spot more unhealthy than Honduras, and when the Englishmen entered the fishing village they found Walker's seventy men lying in the palm huts helpless with fever, and with no stomach to fight British blue-jackets with whom they had no quarrel. Walker inquired of Salmon if he were asking him to surrender to the British or to the Honduranian forces, and twice Salmon assured him, "distinctly and specifically," that he was surrendering to the forces of her Majesty. With this understanding Walker and his men laid down their arms and were conveyed to the *Icarus*. But on arriving at Trujillo, in spite of their protests and demands for trial by a British tribunal, Salmon turned over his prisoners to the Honduranian general. What excuse for this is now given by his descendants in the Salmon family I do not know.

Probably it is a subject they avoid, and, in history, Salmon's version has never been given, which for him, perhaps, is an injustice. But the fact remains that he turned over his white brothers to the mercies of half-Indian, half-negro, savages, who were not allies of Great Britain, and in whose quarrels she had no interest. And Salmon did this, knowing there could be but one end. If he did not know it, his stupidity equalled what now appears to be heartless indifference. So far as to secure pardon for all except the leader and one faithful follower, Colonel Rudler of the famous Phalanx, Salmon did use his authority, and he offered, if Walker would ask as an American citizen, to intercede for him. But Walker, with a distinct sense of loyalty to the country he had conquered, and whose people had honored him with their votes, refused to accept life from the country of his birth, the country that had injured and repudiated him.

Even in his extremity, abandoned and alone on a strip of glaring coral and noisome swamp land, surrounded only by his enemies, he remained true to his ideal.

At thirty-seven life is very sweet, many things still seem possible, and before him, could his life be spared, Walker beheld greater conquests, more power, a new South controlling a Nicaragua canal, a network of busy railroads, great squadrons of merchant vessels, himself emperor of Central America. On the gunboat the gold-braided youth had but to raise his hand, and Walker again would be a free man. But the gold-braided one would render this service only on the condition that Walker would appeal to him as an American; it was not enough that Walker was a human being. The condition Walker could not grant.

"The President of Nicaragua," he said, "is a citizen of Nicaragua."

They led him out at sunrise to a level piece of sand along the beach, and as the priest held the crucifix in front of him he spoke to his executioners in Spanish, simply and gravely: "I die a Roman Catholic. In making war upon you at the invitation of the people of Ruatan I was wrong. Of your people I ask pardon. I accept my punishment with resignation. I would like to think my death will be for the good of society."

From a distance of twenty feet three soldiers fired at him, but, although each shot took effect, Walker was not dead. So, a sergeant stooped, and with a pistol killed the man who would have made him one of an empire of slaves.

Had Walker lived four years longer to exhibit upon the great board of the Civil War his ability as a general, he would, I believe, to-day be ranked as one of America's greatest fighting men.

And because the people of his own day destroyed him is no reason that we should withhold from this American, the greatest of all filibusters, the recognition of his genius.

MAJOR BURNHAM, CHIEF OF SCOUTS

AMONG the Soldiers of Fortune whose stories have been told in this book were men who are no longer living, men who, to the United States, are strangers, and men who were of interest chiefly because in what they attempted they failed.

The subject of this article is none of these. His adventures are as remarkable as any that ever led a small boy to dig behind the barn for buried treasure, or stalk Indians in the orchard. But entirely apart from his adventures he obtains our interest because in what he has attempted he has not failed, because he is one of our own people, one of the earliest and best types of American, and because, so far from being dead and buried, he is at this moment very much alive, and engaged in Mexico in searching for a buried city. For exercise, he is alternately chasing, or being chased by, Yaqui Indians.

In his home in Pasadena, Cal., where sometimes he rests quietly for almost a week at a time, the neighbors know him as "Fred" Burnham. In England the newspapers crowned him "The King of Scouts." Later, when he won an official title, they called him "Major Frederick Russell Burnham, D. S. O."

Some men are born scouts, others by training become

scouts. From his father Burnham inherited his instinct for wood-craft, and to this instinct, which in him is as keen as in a wild deer or a mountain lion, he has added, in the jungle and on the prairie and mountain ranges, years of the hardest, most relentless schooling. In those years he has trained himself to endure the most appalling fatigues, hunger, thirst, and wounds; has subdued the brain to infinite patience, has learned to force every nerve in his body to absolute obedience, to still even the beating of his heart. Indeed, than Burnham no man of my acquaintance to my knowledge has devoted himself to his life's work more earnestly, more honestly, and with such single-mindedness of purpose. To him scouting is as exact a study as is the piano to Paderewski, with the result that to-day what the Pole is to other pianists, the American is to all other "trackers," woodmen, and scouts. He reads "the face of Nature" as you read your morning paper. To him a movement of his horse's ears is as plain a warning as the "Go SLOW" of an automobile sign; and he so saves from ambush an entire troop. In the glitter of a piece of quartz in the firelight he discovers King Solomon's mines. Like the horned cattle, he can tell by the smell of it in the air the near presence of water, and where, glaring in the sun, you can see only a bare kopje, he distinguishes the muzzle of a pompom, the crown of a Boer sombrero, the levelled barrel of a Mauser. He is the Sherlock Holmes of all out-of-doors.

Besides being a scout, he is soldier, hunter, mining expert, and explorer. Within the last ten years the educated instinct that as a younger man taught him to follow the trail of an Indian, or the "spoor" of the Kaffir and the trek wagon, now leads him as a mining expert to the hiding-places of copper, silver, and gold, and, as he advises, great and wealthy syndicates buy or refuse tracts of land in Africa and Mexico as large as the State of New York. As an explorer in the last few years in the course of his expeditions into undiscovered lands, he has added to this little world many thousands of square miles.

Personally, Burnham is as unlike the scout of fiction, and of the Wild West Show, as it is possible for a man to be. He possesses no flowing locks, his talk is not of "greasers," "grizzly b'ars," or "pesky redskins." In fact, because he is more widely and more thoroughly informed, he is much better educated than many who have passed through one of the "Big Three" universities, and his English is as conventional as though he had been brought up on the borders of Boston Common, rather than on the borders of civilization.

In appearance he is slight, muscular, bronzed; with a finely formed square jaw, and remarkable light blue eyes. These eyes apparently never leave yours, but in reality they see everything behind you and about you, above and below you. They tell of him that one day, while out with a patrol on the veldt, he said he had lost the trail and, dismounting, began moving about on his hands and knees, nosing the ground like a bloodhound, and pointing out a trail that led back over the way the force had just marched. When the commanding officer rode up, Burnham said:

"Don't raise your head, sit. On that kopje to the right there is a commando of Boers."

"When did you see them?" asked the officer.

"I see them now," Burnham answered.

"But I thought you were looking for a lost trail?"

"That's what the Boers on the kopje think," said Burnham.

In his eyes, possibly, owing to the uses to which they have been trained, the pupils, as in the eyes of animals that see in the dark, are extremely small. Even in the photographs that accompany this article this feature of his eyes is obvious, and that he can see in the dark the Kaffirs of South Africa firmly believe. In manner he is quiet, courteous, talking slowly but well, and, while without any of that shyness that comes from self-consciousness, extremely modest. Indeed, there could be no better proof of his modesty than the difficulties I have encountered in gathering material for this article, which I have been five years in collecting. And even now, as he reads it by his camp-fire, I can see him squirm with embarrassment.

Burnham's father was a pioneer missionary in a frontier hamlet called Tivoli on the edge of the Indian reserve of Minnesota. He was a stern, severely religious man, born in Kentucky, but educated in New York, where he graduated from the Union Theological Seminary. He was wonderfully skilled in wood-craft. Burnham's mother was a Miss Rebecca Russell of a well-known family in Iowa. She was a woman of great courage, which, in those days on that skirmish line of civilization, was a very necessary virtue; and she was possessed of a most gentle and sweet disposition. That was her gift to her son Fred, who was born on May 11, 1861.

His education as a child consisted in memorizing many verses of the Bible, the "Three R's," and wood-craft. His childhood was strenuous. In his mother's arms he saw the burning of the town of New Ulm, which was the funeral pyre for the women and children of that place when they were massacred by Red Cloud and his braves.

On another occasion Fred's mother fled for her life from the Indians, carrying the boy with her. He was a husky lad, and knowing that if she tried to carry him farther they both would be overtaken, she hid him under a shock of corn. There, the next morning, the Indians having been driven off, she found her son sleeping as soundly as a night watchman. In these Indian wars, and the Civil War which followed, of the families of Burnham and Russell, twenty-two of the men were killed. There is no question that Burnham comes of fighting stock.

In 1870, when Fred was nine years old, his father moved to Los Angeles, Cal., where two years later he died; and for a time for both mother and boy there was poverty, hard and grinding. To relieve this young Burnham acted as a mounted messenger. Often he was in the saddle from twelve to fifteen hours, and even in a land where every one rode well, he gained local fame as a hard rider. In a few years a kind uncle offered to Mrs. Burnham and a younger brother a home in the East, but at the last moment Fred refused to go with them, and chose to make his own way. He was then thirteen years old, and he had determined to be a scout.

At that particular age many boys have set forth determined to be scouts, and are generally brought home the next morning by a policeman. But Burnham, having turned his back on the cities, did not repent. He wandered over Mexico, Arizona, California. He met Indians, bandits, prospectors, hunters of all kinds of big game; and finally a scout who, under General Taylor, had served in the Mexican War. This man took a liking to the boy; and his influence upon him was marked and for his good. He was an educated man, and had carried into the wilderness a few books. In the cabin of this man Burnham read "The Conquest of Mexico and Peru" by Prescott, the lives of Hannibal and Cyrus the Great, of Livingstone the explorer, which first set his thoughts toward Africa, and many technical works on the strategy and tactics of war. He had no experience of military operations on a large scale, but, with the aid of the veteran of the Mexican War, with corn-cobs in the sand in front of the cabin door, he constructed forts and made trenches, redoubts, and traverses. In Burnham's life this seems to have been a very happy period. The big game he hunted and killed he sold for a few dollars to the men of Nadean's freight outfits, which in those days hauled bullion from Cerro Gordo for the man who is now Senator Jones of Nevada.

At nineteen Burnham decided that there were things in this world he should know that could not be gleaned from the earth, trees, and sky; and with the few dollars he had saved he came East. The visit apparently was not a success. The atmosphere of the town in which he went to school was strictly Puritanical, and the townspeople much given to religious discussion. The son of the pioneer missionary found himself unable to subscribe to the formulas which to the others seemed so essential, and he returned to the West with the most bitter feelings, which lasted until he was twenty-one.

"It seems strange now," he once said to me, "but in those times religious questions were as much a part of our daily life as to-day are automobiles, the Standard Oil, and the insurance scandals, and when I went West I was in an unhappy, doubting frame of mind. The trouble was I had no moral anchors; the old ones father had given me were gone, and the time for acquiring new ones had not arrived." This bitterness of heart, or this disappointment, or whatever the state of mind was that the dogmas of the New England town had inspired in the boy from the prairie, made him reckless. For the life he was to lead this was not a handicap. Even as a lad, in a land-grant war in California, he had been under gunfire, and for the next fifteen years he led a life of danger and of daring; and studied in a school of experience than which, for a scout, if his life be spared, there can be none better. Burnham ame out of it a quiet, manly, gentleman. In those fifteen years he roved the West from the Great Divide to Mexico. He fought the Apache Indians for the possession of waterholes, he guarded bullion on stage-coaches, for days rode in pursuit of Mexican bandits and American horse thieves, took part in county-seat fights, in rustler wars, in cattle wars; he was cowboy, miner, deputy-sheriff, and in time throughout the the name of "Fred" Burnham became significant and familiar.

During this period Burnham was true to his boyhood ideal of becoming a scout. It was not enough that by merely living the life around him he was being educated for it. He daily practised and rehearsed those things which some day might mean to himself and others the difference between life and death. To improve his sense of smell he gave up smoking, of which he was extremely fond, nor, for the same reason, does he to this day use tobacco. He accustomed himself also to go with little sleep, and to subsist on the least possible quantity of food. As a deputy-sheriff this educated faculty of not requiring sleep aided him in many important captures. Sometimes he would not strike the trail of the bandit or "bad man" until the other had several days the start of him. But the end was the same; for, while the murderer snatched a few hours' rest by the trail, Burnham, awake and in the saddle, would be closing up the miles between them.

That he is a good marksman goes without telling. At the age of eight his father gave him a rifle of his own, and at twelve, with either a "gun" or a Winchester, he was an expert. He taught himself to use a weapon either in his left or right hand and to shoot, Indian fashion, hanging by one leg from his pony and using it as a cover, and to turn in the saddle and shoot behind him. I once asked him if he really could shoot to the rear with a galloping horse under him and hit a man.

"Well," he said, "maybe not to hit him, but I can come near enough to him to make him decide my pony's so much faster than his that it really isn't worth while to follow me."

Besides perfecting himself in what he tolerantly calls "tricks" of horsemanship and marksmanship, he studied the signs of the trail, forest and prairie, as a sailing-master studies the waves and clouds. The knowledge he gathers from inanimate objects and dumb animals seems little less than miraculous. And when you ask him how he knows these things he always gives you a reason founded on some fact or habit of nature that shows him to be a naturalist, mineralogist, geologist, and botanist, and not merely a seventh son of a seventh son.

In South Africa he would say to the officers: "There are a dozen Boers five miles ahead of us riding Basuto ponies at a trot, and leading five others. If we hurry we should be able to sight them in an hour." At first the officers would smile, but not after a half-hour's gallop, when they would see ahead of them a dozen Boers leading five ponies. In the early days of Salem, Burnham would have been burned as a witch.

When twenty-three years of age he married Miss Blanche Blick, of Iowa. They had known each other from childhood, and her brothers-in-law have been Burnham's aids and companions in every part of Africa and the West. Neither at the time of their marriage nor since did Mrs. Burnham "lay a hand on the bridle rein," as is witnessed by the fact that for nine years after his marriage Burnham continued his career as sheriff, scout, mining prospector. And in 1893, when Burnham and his brother-in-law, Ingram, started for South Africa, Mrs. Burnham went with them, and in every part of South Africa shared her husband's life of travel and danger.

In making this move across the sea, Burnham's original idea was to look for gold in the territory owned by the German East African Company. But as in Rhodesia the first Matabele uprising had broken out, he continued on down the coast, and volunteered for that campaign. This was the real beginning of his fortunes. The "war" was not unlike the Indian fighting of his early days, and although the country was new to him, with the kind of warfare then being waged between the Kaffirs under King Lobengula and the white settlers of the British South Africa Company, the chartered company of Cecil Rhodes, he was intimately familiar.

It does not take big men long to recognize other big men, and Burnham's remarkable work as a scout at once brought him to the notice of Rhodes and Dr. Jameson, who was personally conducting the campaign. The war was their own private war, and to them, at such a crisis in the history of their settlement, a man like Burnham was invaluable.

The chief incident of this campaign, the fame of which rang over all Great Britain and her colonies, was the gallant but hopeless stand made by Major Alan Wilson and his patrol of thirty-four men. It was Burnham's attempt to save these men that made him known from Buluwayo to Cape Town.

King Lobengula and his warriors were halted on one bank of the Shangani River, and on the other Major Forbes, with a picked force of three hundred men, was coming up in pursuit. Although at the moment he did not know it, he also was being pursued by a force of Matabeles, who were gradually surrounding him. At nightfall Major Wilson and a patrol of twelve men, with Burnham and his brother-in-law, Ingram, acting as scouts, were ordered to make a dash into the camp of Lobengula and, if possible, in the confusion of their sudden attack, and under cover of a terrific thunderstorm that was raging, bring him back a prisoner.

With the king in their hands the white men believed the rebellion would collapse. To the number of three thousand the Matabeles were sleeping in a succession of camps, through which the fourteen men rode at a gallop. But in the darkness it was difficult to distinguish the trek wagon of the king, and by the time they found his laager the Matabeles from the other camps through which they had ridden had given the alarm. Through the underbrush from every side the enemy, armed with assegai and elephant guns, charged toward them and spread out to cut off their retreat.

At a distance of about seven hundred yards from the camps there was a giant ant-hill, and the patrol rode toward it. By the aid of the lightning flashes they made their way through a dripping wood and over soil which the rain had turned into thick black mud. When the party drew rein at the ant-hill it was found that of the fourteen three were missing. As the official scout of the patrol and the only one who could see in the dark, Wilson ordered Burnham back to find them. Burnham said he could do so only by feeling the hoof-prints in the mud and that he would like some one with him to lead his pony. Wilson said he would lead it. With his fingers Burnham followed the trail of the eleven horses to where, at right angles, the hoof-prints of the three others separated from it, and so came upon the three men. Still, with nothing but the mud of the jungle to guide him, he brought them back to their comrades. It was this feat that established his reputation among British, Boers, and black men in South Africa.

Throughout the night the men of the patrol lay in the mud holding the reins of their horses. In the jungle about them, they could hear the enemy splashing through the mud, and the swishing sound of the branches as they swept back into place. It was still raining. Just before the dawn there came the sounds of voices and the welcome clatter of accoutrements. The men of the patrol, believing the column had joined them, sprang up rejoicing, but it was only a second patrol, under Captain Borrow, who had been sent forward with twenty men as re-enforcements. They had come in time to share in a glorious immortality.

No sooner had these men joined than the Kaffirs began the attack; and the white men at once learned that they were trapped in a complete circle of the enemy. Hidden by the trees, the Kaffirs fired point-blank, and in a very little time half of Wilson's force was killed or wounded. As the horses were shot down the men used them for breastworks. There was no other shelter. Wilson called Burnham to him and told him he must try and get through the lines of the enemy to Forbes.

"Tell him to come up at once," he said; "we are nearly finished." He detailed a trooper named Gooding and Ingram to accompany Burnham. "One of you may get through," he said. Gooding was but lately out from London, and knew nothing of scouting, so Burnham and Ingram warned him, whether he saw the reason for it or not, to act exactly as they did. The three men had barely left the others before the enemy sprang at them with their spears. In five minutes they were being fired at from every bush. Then followed a remarkable ride, in which Burnham called to his aid all he had learned in thirty years of border warfare. As the enemy rushed after them, the three doubled on their tracks, rode in triple loops, hid in dongas to breathe their horses; and to scatter their pursuers, separated, joined again, and again separated. The enemy followed them to the very bank of the river, where, finding the "drift" covered with the swollen waters, they were forced to swim. They reached the other bank only to find Forbes hotly engaged with another force of the Matabeles.

"I have been sent for re-enforcements," Burnham said to Forbes, "but I believe we are the only survivors of that party." Forbes himself was too hard pressed to give help to Wilson, and Burnham, his errand over, took his place in the column, and began firing upon the new enemy.

Six weeks later the bodies of Wilson's patrol were found lying in a circle. Each of them had been shot many times. A son of Lobengula, who witnessed their extermination, and who in Buluwayo had often heard the Englishmen sing their national anthem, told how the five men who were the last to die stood up and, swinging their hats defiantly, sang "God Save the Queen." The incident will long be recorded in song and story; and in London was reproduced in two theatres, in each of which the man who played "Burnham, the American Scout," as he rode off for re-enforcements, was as loudly cheered by those in the audience as by those on the stage.

Hensman, in his "History of Rhodesia," says: "One hardly knows which to most admire, the men who went on this dangerous errand, through brush swarming with natives, or those who remained behind battling against overwhelming odds."

For his help in this war the Chartered Company presented Burnham with the campaign medal, a gold watch engraved with words of appreciation; and at the suggestion of Cecil Rhodes gave him, Ingram, and the Hon. Maurice Clifford, jointly, a tract of land of three hundred square acres.

After this campaign Burnham led an expedition of ten white men and seventy Kaffirs north of the Zambesi River to explore Barotzeland and other regions to the north of Mashonaland, and to establish the boundaries of the concession given him, Ingram, and Clifford.

In order to protect Burnham on the march the

Chartered Company signed a treaty with the native king of the country through which he wished to travel, by which the king gave him permission to pass freely and guaranteed him against attack.

But Latea, the son of the king, refused to recognize the treaty and sent his young men in great numbers to surround Burnham's camp. Burnham had been instructed to avoid a fight, and was torn between his desire to obey the Chartered Company and to prevent a massacre. He decided to make it a sacrifice either of himself or of Latea. As soon as night fell, with only three companions and a missionary to act as a witness of what occurred, he slipped through the lines of Latea's men, and, kicking down the fence around the prince's hut, suddenly appeared before him and covered him with his rifle.

"Is it peace or war?" Burnham asked. "I have the king your father's guarantee of protection, but your men surround us. I have told my people if they hear shots to open fire. We may all be killed, but you will be the first to die."

The missionary also spoke urging Latea to abide by the treaty. Burnham says the prince seemed much more impressed by the arguments of the missionary than by the fact that he still was covered by Burnham's rifle. Whichever argument moved him, he called off his warriors. On this expedition Burnham discovered the ruins of great granite structures fifteen feet wide, and made entirely without mortar. They were of a period dating before the Phoenicians. He also sought out the ruins described to him by F. C. Selous, the famous hunter, and by Rider Haggard as King Solomon's Mines. Much to the delight of Mr. Haggard, he brought back for him from the mines of his imagination real gold ornaments and a real gold bar.

On this same expedition, which lasted five months, Burnham endured one of the severest hardships of his life. Alone with ten Kaffir boys, he started on a week's journey across the dried-up basin of what once had been a great lake. Water was carried in goat-skins on the heads of the bearers. The boys, finding the bags an unwieldy burden, and believing, with the happy optimism of their race, that Burnham's warnings were needless, and that at a stream they soon could refill the bags, emptied the water on the ground.

The tortures that followed this wanton waste were terrible. Five of the boys died, and after several days, when Burnham found water in abundance, the tongues of the others were so swollen that their jaws could not meet.

On this trip Burnham passed through a region ravaged by the "sleeping sickness," where his nostrils were never free from the stench of dead bodies, where in some of the villages, as he expressed it, "the hyenas were mangy with overeating, and the buzzards so gorged they could not move out of our way." From this expedition he brought back many ornaments of gold manufactured before the Christian era, and made several valuable maps of hitherto uncharted regions. It was in recognition of the information gathered by him on this trip that he was elected a Fellow of the Royal Geographical Society.

He returned to Rhodesia in time to take part in the second Matabele rebellion. This was in 1896. By now Burnham was a very prominent member of the "vortrekers" and pioneers at Buluwayo, and Sir Frederick Carrington, who was in command of the forces, attached him to his staff. This second outbreak was a more serious uprising than the one of 1893, and as it was evident the forces of the Chartered Company could not handle it, imperial troops were sent to assist them. But with even their aid the war dragged on until it threatened to last to the rainy season, when the troops must have gone into winter quarters. Had they done so, the cost of keeping them would have fallen on the Chartered Company, already a sufferer in pocket from the ravages of the rinderpest and the expenses of the investigation which followed the Jameson raid.

Accordingly, Carrington looked about for some measure by which he could bring the war to an immediate end.

It was suggested to him by a young Colonial, named Armstrong, the Commissioner of the district, that this could be done by destroying the "god," or high priest, Umlimo, who was the chief inspiration of the rebellion.

This high priest had incited the rebels to a general massacre of women and children, and had given them confidence by promising to strike the white soldiers blind and to turn their bullets into water. Armstrong had discovered the secret hiding-place of Umlimo, and Carrington ordered Burnham to penetrate the enemy's lines, find the god, capture him, and if that were not possible to destroy him.

The adventure was a most desperate one. Umlimo was secreted in a cave on the top of a huge kopje. At the base of this was a village where were gathered two regiments, of a thousand men each, of his fighting men.

For miles around this village the country was patrolled by roving bands of the enemy.

Against a white man reaching the cave and returning, the chances were a hundred to one, and the difficulties of the journey are illustrated by the fact that Burnham and Armstrong were unable to move faster than at the rate of a mile an hour. In making the last mile they consumed three hours. When they reached the base of the kopje in which Umlimo was hiding, they concealed their ponies in a clump of bushes, and on hands and knees began the ascent.

Directly below them lay the village, so close that they could smell the odors of cooking from the huts, and hear, rising drowsily on the hot, noonday air, voices of the warriors. For minutes at a time they lay as motionless as the granite bowlders around or squirmed and crawled over loose stones which a miss of hand or knee would have dislodged and sent clattering into the village. After an hour of this tortuous climbing the cave suddenly opened before them, and they beheld Umlimo. Burnham recognized that to take him alive from his stronghold was an impossibility, and that even they themselves would leave the place was equally doubtful. So, obeying orders, he fired, killing the man who had boasted he would turn the bullets of his enemies into water. The echo of the shot aroused the village as would a stone hurled into an ant-heap. In an instant the veldt below was black with running men, and as, concealment being no longer possible, the white men rose to fly a great shout of anger told them they were discovered. At the same moment two women, returning from a stream where they had gone for water, saw the ponies, and ran screaming to give the alarm. The race that followed lasted two hours, for so quickly did the Kaffirs spread out on every side that it was impossible for Burnham to gain ground in any one direction, and he was forced to dodge, turn, and double. At one time the white men were driven back to the very kopje from which the race had started.

But in the end they evaded assegai and gunfire, and in safety reached Buluwayo. This exploit was one of the chief factors in bringing the war to a close. The Matabeles, finding their leader was only a mortal like themselves, and so could not, as he had promised, bring miracles to their aid, lost heart, and when Cecil Rhodes in person made overtures of peace, his terms were accepted. During the hard days of the siege, when rations were few and bad, Burnham's little girl, who had been the first white child born in Buluwayo, died of fever and lack of proper food. This with other causes led him to leave Rhodesia and return to California. It is possible he then thought he had forever turned his back on South Africa, but, though he himself had departed, the impression he had made there remained behind him.

Burnham did not rest long in California. In Alaska the hunt for gold had just begun, and, the old restlessness seizing him, he left Pasadena and her blue skies, tropical plants, and trolley-car strikes for the new raw land of the Klondike. With Burnham it has always been the place that is being made, not the place in being, that attracts. He has helped to make straight the ways of several great communities - Arizona, California, Rhodesia, Alaska, and Uganda. As he once said: "It is the constructive side of frontier life that most appeals to me, the building up of a country, where you see the persistent drive and force of the white man; when the place is finally settled I don't seem to enjoy it very long."

In Alaska he did much prospecting, and, with a sled and only two dogs, for twenty-four days made one long fight against snow and ice, covering six hundred miles. In mining in Alaska he succeeded well, but against the country he holds a constant grudge, because it kept him out of the fight with Spain. When war was declared he was in the wilds and knew nothing of it, and though on his return to civilization he telegraphed Colonel Roosevelt volunteering for the Rough Riders, and at once started south, by the time he had reached Seattle the war was over.

Several times has he spoken to me of how bitterly he regretted missing this chance to officially fight for his country. That he had twice served with English forces made him the more keen to show his loyalty to his own people.

That he would have been given a commission in the Rough Riders seems evident from the opinion President Roosevelt has publicly expressed of him.

"I know Burnham," the President wrote in 1901. "He is a scout and a hunter of courage and ability, a man totally without fear, a sure shot, and a fighter. He is the ideal scout, and when enlisted in the military service of any country he is bound to be of the greatest benefit."

The truth of this Burnham was soon to prove.

In 1899 he had returned to the Klondike, and in

January of 1900 had been six months in Skagway. In that same month Lord Roberts sailed for Cape Town to take command of the army, and with him on his staff was Burnham's former commander, Sir Frederick, now Lord, Carrington. One night as the ship was in the Bay of Biscay, Carrington was talking of Burnham and giving instances of his marvellous powers as a "tracker."

"He is the best scout we ever had in South Africa!" Carrington declared.

"Then why don't we get him back there?" said Roberts.

What followed is well known.

From Gibraltar a cable was sent to Skagway, offering Burnham the position, created especially for him, of chief of scouts of the British army in the field.

Probably never before in the history of wars has one nation paid so pleasant a tribute to the abilities of a man of another nation.

The sequel is interesting. The cablegram reached Skagway by the steamer *City of Seattle*. The purser left it at the post-office, and until two hours and a half before the steamer was listed to start on her return trip, there it lay. Then Burnham, in asking for his mail, received it. In two hours and a half he had his family, himself, and his belongings on board the steamer, and had started on his half-around-the-world journey from Alaska to Cape Town.

A Skagway paper of January 5, 1900, published the day after Burnham sailed, throws a side light on his character. After telling of his hasty departure the day before, and of the high compliment that had been paid to "a prominent Skagwayan," it adds: "Although Mr. Burnham has lived in Skagway since last August, and has been North for many months, he has said little of his past, and few have known that he is the man famous over the world as 'the American scout' of the Matabele wars."

Many a man who went to the Klondike did not, for reasons best known to himself, talk about his past. But it is characteristic of Burnham that, though he lived there two years, his associates did not know, until the British Government snatched him from among them, that he had not always been a prospector like themselves.

I was on the same ship that carried Burnham the latter half of his journey, from Southampton to Cape Town, and every night for seventeen nights was one of a group of men who shot questions at him. And it was interesting to see a fellow-countryman one had heard praised so highly so completely make good. It was not as though he had a credulous audience of commercial tourists. Among the officers who each evening gathered around him were Colonel Gallilet of the Egyptian cavalry, Captain Frazer commanding the Scotch Gillies, Captain Mackie of Lord Roberts's staff, each of whom was later killed in action; Colonel Sir Charles Hunter of the Royal Rifles, Major Bagot, Major Lord Dudley, and Captain Lord Valentia. Each of these had either held command in border fights in India or the Sudan or had hunted big game, and the questions each asked were the outcome of his own experience and observation.

Not for a single evening could a faker have submitted to the midnight examination through which they put Burnham and not have exposed his ignorance. They wanted to know what difference there is in a column of dust raised by cavalry and by trek wagons, how to tell whether a horse that has passed was going at a trot or a gallop, the way to throw a diamond hitch, how to make a fire without at the same time making a target of yourself, how - why - what - and how?

And what made us most admire Burnham was that when he did not know he at once said so.

Within two nights he had us so absolutely at his mercy that we would have followed him anywhere; anything he chose to tell us, we would have accepted. We were ready to believe in flying foxes, flying squirrels, that wild turkeys dance quadrilles - even that you must never sleep in the moonlight. Had he demanded: "Do you believe in vampires?" we would have shouted "Yes." To ask that a scout should on an ocean steamer prove his ability was certainly placing him under a severe handicap.

As one of the British officers said: "It's about as fair a game as though we planted the captain of this ship in the Sahara Desert, and told him to prove he could run a ten-thousand-ton liner."

Burnham continued with Lord Roberts to the fall of Pretoria, when he was invalided home.

During the advance north he was a hundred times inside the Boer laagers, keeping Headquarters Staff daily informed of the enemy's movements; was twice captured and twice escaped.

He was first captured while trying to warn the British from the fatal drift at Thaba'nchu. When reconnoitring alone in the morning mist he came upon the Boers hiding on the banks of the river, toward which the English were even then advancing. The Boers were moving all about him, and cut him off from his own side. He had to choose between abandoning the English to the trap or signalling to them, and so exposing himself to capture. With the red kerchief the scouts carried for that purpose he wigwagged to the approaching soldiers to turn back, that the enemy were awaiting them. But the column, which was without an advance guard, paid no attention to his signals and plodded steadily on into the ambush, while Burnham was at once made prisoner. In the fight that followed he pretended to receive a wound in the knee and bound it so elaborately that not even a surgeon would have disturbed the carefully arranged bandages. Limping heavily and groaning with pain, he was placed in a trek wagon with the officers who really were wounded, and who, in consequence, were not closely guarded. Burnham told them who he was and, as he intended to escape, offered to take back to head-quarters their names or any messages they might wish to send to their people. As twenty yards behind the wagon in which they lay was a mounted guard, the officers told him escape was impossible. He proved otherwise. The trek wagon was drawn by sixteen oxen and driven by a Kaffir boy. Later in the evening, but while it still was moonlight, the boy descended from his seat and ran forward to belabor the first spans of oxen. This was the opportunity for which Burnham had been waiting.

Slipping quickly over the driver's seat, he dropped between the two "wheelers" to the disselboom, or tongue, of the trek wagon. From this he lowered himself and fell between the legs of the oxen on his back in the road. In an instant the body of the wagon had passed over him, and while the dust still hung above the trail he rolled rapidly over into the ditch at the side of the road and lay motionless.

It was four days before he was able to re-enter the British lines, during which time he had been lying in the open veldt, and had subsisted on one biscuit and two handfuls of "mealies," or what we call Indian corn.

Another time when out scouting he and his Kaffir boy while on foot were "jumped" by a Boer commando and forced to hide in two great ant-hills. The Boers went into camp on every side of them, and for two days, unknown to themselves, held Burnham a prisoner. Only at night did he and the Cape boy dare to crawl out to breathe fresh air and to eat the food tablets they carried in their pockets. On five occasions was Burnham sent into the Boer lines with dynamite cartridges to blow up the railroad over which the enemy was receiving supplies and ammunition. One of these expeditions nearly ended his life.

On June 2, 1901, while trying by night to blow up the line between Pretoria and Delagoa Bay, he was surrounded by a party of Boers and could save himself only by instant flight. He threw himself Indian fashion along the back of his pony, and had all but got away when a bullet caught the horse and, without even faltering in its stride, it crashed to the ground dead, crushing Burnham beneath it and knocking him senseless. He continued unconscious for twenty-four hours, and when he came to, both friends and foes had departed. Bent upon carrying out his orders, although suffering the most acute agony, he crept back to the railroad and destroyed it. Knowing the explosion would soon bring the Boers, on his hands and knees he crept to an empty kraal, where for two days and nights he lay insensible. At the end of that time he appreciated that he was sinking and that unless he found aid he would die.

Accordingly, still on his hands and knees, he set forth toward the sound of distant firing. He was indifferent as to whether it came from the enemy or his own people, but, as it chanced, he was picked up by a patrol of General Dickson's Brigade, who carried him to Pretoria. There the surgeons discovered that in his fall he had torn apart the muscles of the stomach and burst a blood-vessel. That his life was saved, so they informed him, was due only to the fact that for three days he had been without food. Had he attempted to digest the least particle of the "staff of life " he would have surely died. His injuries were so serious that he was ordered home.

On leaving the army he was given such hearty thanks and generous rewards as no other American ever received from the British War Office. He was promoted to the rank of major, presented with a large sum of money, and from Lord Roberts received a personal letter of thanks and appreciation.

In part the Field-Marshal wrote: "I doubt if any other man in the force could have successfully carried out the thrilling enterprises in which from time to time you have been engaged, demanding as they did the training of a lifetime, combined with exceptional courage, caution, and powers of endurance." On his arrival in England he was commanded to dine with the Queen and spend the night at Osborne, and a few months later, after her death, King Edward created him a member of the Distinguished Service Order, and personally presented him with the South African medal with five bars, and the cross of the D. S. 0. While recovering his health Burnham, with Mrs. Burnham, was "passed on" by friends he had made in the army from country house to country house; he was made the guest of honor at city banquets, with the Duke of Rutland rode after the Belvoir hounds, and in Scotland made mild excursions after grouse. But after six months of convalescence he was off again, this time to the hinterland of Ashanti, on the west coast of Africa, where he went in the interests of a syndicate to investigate a concession for working gold mines.

With his brother-in-law, J. C. Blick, he marched and rowed twelve hundred miles, and explored the Volta River, at that date so little visited that in one day's journey they counted eleven hippopotamuses. In July, 1901, he returned from Ashanti, and a few months later an unknown but enthusiastic admirer asked in the House of Commons if it were true Major Burnham had applied for the post of Instructor of Scouts at Aldershot. There is no such post, and Burnham had not applied for any other post. To the Timer he wrote: "I never have thought myself competent to teach Britons how to fight, or to act as an instructor with officers who have fought in every corner of the world. The question asked in Parliament was entirely without my knowledge, and I deeply regret that it was asked." A few months later, with Mrs. Burnham and his younger son, Bruce, he journeyed to East Africa as director of the East African Syndicate.

During his stay there the *African Review* said of him: "Should East Africa ever become a possession for

England to be proud of, she will owe much of her prosperity to the brave little band that has faced hardships and dangers in discovering her hidden resources. Major Burnham has chosen men from England, Ireland, the United States, and South Africa for sterling qualities, and they have justified his choice. Not the least like a hero is the retiring, diffident little major himself, though a finer man for a friend or a better man to serve under would not be found in the five continents."

Burnham explored a tract of land larger than Germany, penetrating a thousand miles through a country, never before visited by white men, to the borders of the Congo Basin. With him he had twenty white men and five hundred natives. The most interesting result of the expedition was the discovery of a lake forty-nine miles square, composed almost entirely of pure carbonate of soda, forming a snowlike crust so thick that on it the men could cross the lake.

It is the largest, and when the railroad is built - the Uganda Railroad is now only eighty-eight miles distant - it will be the most valuable deposit of carbonate of soda ever found.

A year ago, in the interests of John Hays Hammond, the distinguished mining engineer of South Africa and this country, Burnham went to Sonora, Mexico, to find a buried city and to open up mines of copper and silver.

Besides seeking for mines, Hammond and Burnham, with Gardner Williams, another American who also made his fortune in South Africa, are working together on a scheme to import to this country at their own expense many species of South African deer.

The South African deer is a hardy animal and can live where the American deer cannot, and the idea in importing him is to prevent big game in this country from passing away. They have asked Congress to set aside for these animals a portion of the forest reserve. Already Congress has voted toward the plan $15,000, and President Roosevelt is one of its most enthusiastic supporters.

We cannot leave Burnham in better hands than those of Hammond and Gardner Williams. Than these three men the United States has not sent to British Africa any Americans of whom she has better reason to be proud. Such men abroad do for those at home untold good. They are the real ambassadors of their country.

The last I learned of Burnham is told in the snapshot of him which accompanies this article, and which shows him, barefoot, in the Yaqui River, where he has gone, perhaps, to conceal his trail from the Indians. It came a month ago in a letter which said briefly that when the picture was snapped the expedition was "trying to cool off." There his narrative ended. Promising as it does adventures still to come, it seems a good place in which to leave him.

Meanwhile, you may think of Mrs. Burnham after a year in Mexico keeping the house open for her husband's return to Pasadena, and of their first son, Roderick, studying woodcraft with his father, forestry with Gifford Pinchot, and playing right guard on the freshman team at the University of California.

But Burnham himself we will leave "cooling off " in

the Yaqui River, maybe, with Indians hunting for him along the banks. And we need not worry about him. We know they will not catch him.

www.ingramcontent.com/pod-product-compliance
Lightning Source LLC
Chambersburg PA
CBHW020001050426
42450CB00005B/276